On Steam

BRITISH STANDARD GAUGE RAILWAYS
RESCUED FROM EXTINCTION

GRANADA
London Toronto Sydney New York

The *Sir Nigel Gresley* climbing the last miles to Aisgill summit, on an enthusiasts' round trip from Middlesbrough, via Newcastle, Carlisle, Leeds and York, and so back to Tees-side. The famous 'A4' hauled the train from Carlisle to York   *David Eatwell*

On Steam

BRITISH STANDARD GAUGE RAILWAYS
RESCUED FROM EXTINCTION

O. S. Nock
B Sc, C Eng, F I C E, F I Mech E

Granada Publishing Limited
Frogmore, St Albans, Herts AL2 2NF
and
36 Golden Square, London W1R 4AH
866 United Nations Plaza, New York, NY 10017,
    USA
117 York Street, Sydney, NSW 2000, Australia
100 Skyway Avenue, Rexdale, Ontario M9W 3A6,
    Canada
61 Beach Road, Auckland, New Zealand

Published by Granada Publishing 1982

British Library Cataloguing in Publication Data
Nock, O.S.
    On steam.
    1. Railroads, Local and light—Great
    Britain—History
    I. Title
385′.0941   HE3816

ISBN 0−246−11736−2

Typeset by Style Photosetting Ltd,
Southborough, Tunbridge Wells, Kent

Designed by Stonecastle Graphics,
Tunbridge Wells, Kent

Printed in Great Britain by
Mackays of Chatham, Kent

Granada®
Granada Publishing®

Contents

PREFACE

Rather more than twenty years ago I wrote a book entitled *Branch Lines*. The great modernization plan of British Railways had not long been launched, and the book was a nostalgic memory of what the country branch lines were like. Modernization, with the implanting of diesel multiple-unit trains, instead of steam, fore-shadowed a complete change in their character, and my book tried to present a last look, as it were, before the great change began. My last paragraph read:

One last thought: the rural branch line of the late-Victorian times was an institution. Is there no chance of one such line, in beautiful country, being preserved under the auspices of the Commission as a working period show-piece; a show-piece to which, and on which, excursions could be run? It would be a delight to the visitors, and an enrichment and a focus point for that keen interest in the railway historical relics that are now scattered rather haphazardly in many parts of the country.

That book of mine had not been very long in circulation before it became evident that the great modernization plan was not working out very well. The railways were losing more and more money every year; and while the anti-steam faction in the top echelons of management continued to chorus, with pitiful naivety, 'We shall be all right once we get rid of steam', there were others who realized that the trouble lay far deeper. In 1962 the government of the day, under Harold Macmillan, with Ernest Marples as Minister of Transport, brought in new legislation that replaced the unwieldy two-tier top level organization of British Transport Commission and Railway Executive, and set up instead, as from New Year's Day 1963, the British Railways Board, with Dr Richard Beeching as its first chairman. His mandate could not have been simpler: 'make the railways pay'. He brought to the task the clear brain and coldly analytical mind of a professional scientist of the very highest order, and in such conditions the vast majority of the branch lines became threatened not with losing their old character, but with complete obliteration.

Enthusiasts of every estate were as horrified as the railwaymen who stood to lose their jobs. Could nothing be done? While the successful preservation of the narrow gauge Talyllyn and Festiniog railways showed what could be done in one direction, it was another matter where stan-dard gauge branches and subsidiary lines were threatened. Enthusiasts in many parts of the country, often without any true realization of what their proposals would involve, tried to launch preservation schemes for this or that branch line, while a simultaneous movement sought to save many of the closures by the formation of a Branch Line Re-invigoration Society. Much has happened since those disturbing days of the early 1960s. Some historic and picturesque lines have been preserved and restored to operating condition, nearly all relying for the most part on volunteer labour. Generally there has been no attempt to provide an all-the-year-round commercial service, and operation takes the form of seasonal running only, when the many volunteers take part of their annual leave helping in diverse ways.

A very large number of locomotives, saved from the scrap heap, have found their way to one or another of these railways, not all in working condition, and generally in far greater numbers than would be required to work even the attenuated service now offered. One private railway, for example, has no more than five miles of line open, yet owns twenty-four steam locomotives and two internal combustion driven units. Of course the preservation of historic and favourite locomotives is a great activity in itself, and it is natural that units saved from destruction have tended to congregate at places where there is a stretch of line on which they can be run; but steam locomotives can be a wasting asset, and saving them from the scrap heap does not mean that they are going to remain even in the state of decrepitude in which they were rescued.

The rehabilitation and running of a number of branch lines, and at least two sections of main line, represents a remarkable sociological as well as technical achievement. Most of us have at varying times in our lives felt an urge to 'play trains', but there is mighty little of 'play' in the weekends of toil that so many volunteers devote to the well-being of the private railways of Britain. Few are qualified as engine drivers, or even as firemen, and it is a hard slog for those maintaining the track in good order, or giving diligent attention to the thousand and one humdrum, but very necessary, jobs to be done on locomotives and coaching stock in the sheds or works. They have the satisfaction of knowing that by their corporate effort a great deal of pleasure is given to those who come to see the railway and ride in the trains.

When I was asked to write a book about the private railways of Britain I was glad that an opportunity had come my way of paying a tribute to those who, in this materialistic age, are happy to do hard manual work as volunteers. At the same time, however, I must make it clear that this is not a handbook or a precise statistical survey of what is to be seen. Nor do I claim to have covered *all* the private railways in this country. There is no mention of the largest private railway, that operated by the Manchester Ship Canal Company, which has some fifty miles of line open, and operates entirely with diesel locomotives. But this is a wholly professional affair, and this book is primarily concerned with lines that were once part of the British Railways network and have been rescued from extinction, if not from memory, by enthusiastic and erudite amateurs — amateurs only in that they do the job for love, while applying very professional standards to the task.

Without exception they are working against a background of fascinating railway history, on which I have touched in referring to present activities. I have, indeed, hinted as to how present activities might develop the historical aspects what is now displayed and enacted, so that these hard-won enterprises could become living memorials to the nineteenth-century age of railways, in the country where the industry was born.

My thanks are due to David & Charles Ltd for permitting me to quote the passage from my book *Engine 6000* in Chapter 7.

How It All Began

At one time, of course, all the railways of Britain were privately owned, and most of them earned reasonably good dividends for their shareholders. They were common carriers. They could not pick and choose; they had to take whatever traffic was offered to them. But in those far-off days before World War I, when railways were the pre-eminent form of transport for passengers, general merchandise, heavy minerals and all else, there was no detailed costing to reveal which particular traffics were profitable and which were not; the whole business was lumped together, and generally the good significantly outbalanced the bad. It needed the advent of an outstanding economist, Sir Josiah Stamp on the L M S, to initiate the process of individual costing to reveal where financial weaknesses existed. This principle, which some of the diehards sometimes referred to as bureaucracy-run-mad, was first applied to locomotive running expenses; but in the straitened economic circumstances of the 1930s it became clear to the top management of the L M S, and in due course to the other major 'Group' companies, that the poor showing of the subsidiary and feeder services — not only on the branch lines — was to a considerable extent due to the statutory conditions in which they had to operate. These conditions had been established, and made law, when railways had the field to themselves. In the 1930s they found themselves fighting a desperate battle for survival against road haulage interests, and hamstrung by outdated legislation.

The celebrated campaign for a 'square deal', waged jointly by the four main line railway companies, was bitterly opposed by the road haulage interests, and by all those who never failed to let an opportunity pass for taking a knock at the railways; and it had made little headway when the international situation in 1939 began to deteriorate so rapidly as to obscure all, or nearly all, domestic issues. The railways were called upon to make a mammoth effort during the war, which duty they faithfully discharged; but immediately it was over the General Election of 1945 made it certain that they would very soon be nationalized, and for a time the whole situation became one of party politics rather than of the economics of transport. With the end of Lease-Lend aid from the USA, and the inevitable continuance of petrol rationing, the railways had to carry on in a situation of deep austerity. In such circumstances there was no justification, or funds, for capital expenditure on more modern forms of motive power; steam traction had to carry on. It was not until the country was at last climbing out of the 'slough of despond', and the Modernization Plan was launched, during the time of Sir Brian Robertson's Chairmanship of the Railway

Executive, that a 'square deal' of a materialistic nature loomed up for the railways.

This gigantic spending spree, which many of the most senior non-technical men glibly imagined would reverse the adverse financial position once steam traction was eliminated, did not take into account the areas of weakness and strength. The branch lines were to get diesel multiple-unit sets instead of short steam trains hauled by little tank engines; one-time competitive routes remained, faintly glamorized by the addition of high-sounding titles for some of the principal express trains. And the bank balance dipped still further into the red. It became clear that gallant soldiers are not necessarily the ideal people to rescue an ailing national railway system. The government of the day determined upon a major reconstruction at top level, and brought in Dr Beeching, a scientist from ICI, to head the new organization. His mandate was to make the railways pay. His approach to the whole problem of British Railways was closely analogous to the methods Sir Josiah Stamp had used in dealing with the problems of the L M S in the 1930s. Neither had reached his respective very eminent position in railway service, and in consequence neither had any preconceived ideas as a result of previous training or experience. They came to the railways entirely fresh. The difference was that while Stamp had to work within the framework of Victorian legislation, Beeching had, very largely, a free hand.

In the world of the railway enthusiast some hard things have been said about Beeching. He has been referred to as 'The Butcher', wielding an inexorable axe. But the railway enthusiast is apt to look at railways in a different light from those who have to run them, and still more so from those whose bounden duty is try and make them pay. Gerard Fiennes, in his stirring and outspoken book *I Tried to Run a Railway,* constantly refers to Beeching as 'the great and good Doctor', and there is no doubt that Beeching brought an impartial and fiercely critical brain to bear upon railway operation. At the time of his appointment the loyalties and partisan sentiments towards the old railway companies were wearing thin among the more forward-looking members of the staff, and in the cold light of economic necessity many of them, looking at the British railway network as a whole, realized that some considerable pruning was urgently necessary. This, to the dedicated railwayman's point of view, did not involve the lopping off of so many branch lines, but the elimination of what were obviously duplicate facilities that in many cases dated back to the most vigorously competitive days of the nineteenth century, when Parliament itself set the veto on anything in the proposed mergers that looked like establishing a monopoly. It did not need detailed financial surveys to show that a high proportion of the branch lines were money-losers; but they were regarded as feeders of useful traffic to the main stems.

Furthermore, the railways were national property, and had a social as well as an economic function to discharge. Their vital role had been shown in two world wars, and despite all that has happened since they provide facilities that road haulage cannot entirely replace. Nevertheless Beeching and his minions set about their task with a vigour that appalled everyone who had the British Railways at heart. It was not only that many men were likely to lose their jobs, and whole communities to lose their railway, but among high-ranking professionals it was felt that the vassals of the 'great and good Doctor' were applying a somewhat negative approach to the job of making the railways pay. It seemed that the principle being formulated by these 'assistant butchers' was that if a line did not pay it should be closed down — full stop! There was no investigation into why it was uneconomic, and no attempt to find out how things could be improved and the adverse balance reversed. As the full extent of the intended closures was revealed the bewilderment, shock and virtual disbelief gave place to anger that was voiced in countless protests. In certain instances, however, when men from the Ministry came to listen to arguments against closure, the cases were not strengthened when it was observed that the majority of the protesters had travelled to the meetings not by train but in their own cars!

Some of the bigger schemes were quite horrific in their extent. One proposed that the entire railway system north and west of Inverness should be abandoned. This would have involved the one-time strategic lifelines to Wick and Thurso, and from Dingwall to the Kyle of Lochalsh. Another scheme was to terminate the railways of the West of England at Plymouth. Others that could be more easily justified did eventually take place. However much the romantics amongst us may have regretted it, two wild routes athwart the northern Pennines had to go. One was the westward extension of the Stockton and Darlington, a one-time independent concern with the unlikely name of the South Durham and Lancashire Union Railway, which at Stainmore topped the crest of the mountain range at a summit point only a few feet short of the highest level attained by any railway in England. Over this steeply graded route there was at one time a profitable reciprocal traffic between Tees-side and the iron ore districts of Furness, via Tebay and the connecting link between the London and North Western main line at Hincaster Junction and the Furness line proper at Arnside. Eastbound went the trains of iron ore, and in return were carried heavy loads of coke for the blast furnaces. But when Beeching came upon the scene this traffic had dwindled, and the passenger business was negligible.

Further south, the line that branched westwards from the East Coast main line at Northallerton was even less likely to survive. It straggled through a wholly rural and upland district to make an end-on junction with a branch of the Midland Railway at Hawes. Yet at one time the passenger business on this line was such that at least one of the Midland 'Scotch Expresses' used to stop at Hawes Junction, the wild and lonely main line connecting point, to pick up and set down traffic. While in Beeching's day any through freight traffic that might have struggled over Stainmore could have been sent from Tees-side to Barrow-in-Furness by the equally circuitous, if somewhat longer route via Leeds and Skipton — 160 miles from Middlesbrough to Barrow, against 111 miles via Tebay — there was no need to consider possible alternatives to the direct line from Northallerton to Hawes Junction, for the business had virtually ceased to exist.

Two very important main line closures need more than a mere passing reference, because they both led to developments in the general context of this book. The southward extension of the one-time Manchester, Sheffield and Lincolnshire Railway, from Annesley, twelve miles north of Nottingham, to link up with the Metropolitan Railway, and so provide a new and highly competitive route from the Midlands into London, can, in retrospect, be seen as one of those nineteenth-century railway enterprises that were not really justified — even in the boundless spirit of enterprise that then prevailed. Rugby, Leicester, Loughborough, Nottingham and Sheffield all had excellent existing services to and from London, and in the Beeching era, the Great Central line immediately became suspect. It carried a considerable amount of freight, but the planners sought ways of diverting this by one or another of the several alternative routes that were readily available.

The other important closure was of the Somerset and Dorset Joint Line, from Bath to Bournemouth, an exceedingly difficult line to operate, single tracked for much of its length, and infested with such severe gradients as to make overall running times, even of the most important express trains, unrealistic in the context of modern requirements.

In the face of the threatened closures a spate of branch line preservation schemes was launched. At first the projects were all very confused and unconnected. Individuals wrote to the railway press stating that they would like to see this or that line preserved, and asking for support. Others concentrated upon locomotives of their own particular fancy. In the early days of nationalization, long before the advent of Beeching, the Railway Executive had drawn up a list of

locomotives to be preserved, not more than one of a design; but in the haste that followed the Beeching proposals and the inexorable drive to get rid of steam traction as quickly as possible, many more individual locomotives were singled out for preservation, by funds raised by independent appeals. Some were lifted literally from the scrap yard at Barry, others were purchased as they were withdrawn from active revenue-earning service on British Railways. The question quickly arose as to what should be done with these locomotives, some of which were of the largest and most modern types. Structural considerations precluded their use on some of the branch lines that were being taken over, and they remained on British Railways property involving their new owners in rental charges.

At that time there were certain members of the British Railways Board (not Beeching himself) who did everything possible to obstruct the retention, even in private hands, of any relics of the steam era — locomotives or otherwise. To hamper activities, lengths of track leading to the condemned branches were in some cases removed, and preservation activity was regarded as the work of a few nostalgic fanatics. It is, however, very important to recall that this attitude was not that of very many professional railwaymen. They were deeply cognizant of the uprooting, dissolution, and premature destruction of equipment that had very far to go before reaching the end of its economic life; but they had their own hands full loyally carrying out the programme of transition and contraction which their masters had decreed should be driven through in a tearing hurry. As with the Light Brigade at Balaclava theirs was not to reason why. So far as the scrapping of locomotives was concerned their carefully considered recommendations, based on a century of hard experiences, were overruled by the politico-

neophytes. That the mighty transition from steam to diesel was carried through with so little upheaval and train service disruption was to the lasting honour of the engineers.

When it became apparent that the programme of replacement was going to involve the withdrawal of many hundreds of relatively new locomotives, there developed a veritable rash of schemes to save engines that had seen little service, and which could reasonably be expected to be in good condition. In the schemes that were springing up everywhere to save branch lines the immediate intention was to keep steam trains running, and these modern locomotives naturally seemed the most likely for the job. The fact that they would not accord with their new surroundings was in this first confused period somewhat apart from the point. Neither was the prospect of using very large modern main line locomotives on hitherto sleepy branch lines considered odd. The main thing was to save some of them, and to have track on which to run them.

The enthusiasts who plunged headlong into these activities, although working in their own immediate interests and usually quite parochially, were in fact laying the foundations for a chain of loving memorials to the age of steam. However much the modernists may poke fun at those who worship at the shrine of the steam locomotive, the steam railway age to future historians will unquestionably be seen as one of the great evolving epochs in human history, and there is every reason for trying to preserve as many examples of it as we can. The million-dollar question, however, after some twenty years of experience, is whether the resources available are being deployed to the best advantage and in a way that will be of lasting value to the history of this vital form of industrial archaeology.

Twenty years ago, given the attitude of the most senior management of British Railways at the start of the preservation movement, it would have been scarcely credible that steam-hauled rail tours would be authorized over British Railways tracks on so extensive a scale. It is now known that such

The author on the footplate of the G E R 0-6-0 No. 564 at Weybourne, North Norfolk Railway, May 1978

Brian Fisher

tours are good business, and at least one region has organized steam-hauled tours of its own. As British Railways owns no steam locomotives, the motive power has to be hired from one or other of the private owners of preserved locomotives. This activity has brought into prominence another aspect of preservation activity, namely the privately managed Steam Centres, where numbers of steam locomotives are based and maintained in a condition acceptable to the highest standards of British Railways and of the Ministry of Transport for hauling passenger trains on British Railways' tracks.

BLUEBELL

Until the Beeching axe fell there were three ways by which one could travel from East Croydon, via Oxted, to Brighton. The first was via Edenbridge, Crowborough, Uckfield and Lewes, while the second took the 'middle way' via East Grinstead and Horsted Keynes to join the first route at Culver Junction. The third followed the second route as far as Horsted Keynes and then cut westward through Ardingly to join the Brighton main line at Copyhold Junction, north of Haywards Heath. The middle route began as the Lewes, East Grinstead and London Railway, promoted in 1876; but from its opening in 1882 it was operated by the London, Brighton and South Coast Railway. In the placid Sussex countryside one could hardly expect there to be a great deal of traffic for *three* parallel routes, even though most of it was undoubtedly local; while from Eridge southwards there was the fourth route, the celebrated 'Cuckoo' line, through Mayfield and Hailsham to join the east-west coastal route at Polegate. Yet, believe it or not, in the years immediately before World War II there were about a dozen trains per day in each direction between Brighton and East Grinstead, via Lewes.

It is easy to understand how enthusiasts of the old Brighton Railway felt when news came of the impending closures. In pre-grouping days the line probably had more supporters, in relation to its size and extent, than any other railway in the country, surpassing those of the London and North Western, and the Great Western. It was largely among Brighton enthusiasts that the Stephenson Locomotive Society had its birth, and interest penetrated into the most remote and secluded of the branch lines as well as on the main lines, or in the teeming commuter network of the South London suburbs. For on the country branches the old Stroudley engines were still at work, albeit rebuilt with Marsh boilers and decked in his smart, though less glamorous, livery of dark umber instead of yellow ochre. But the atmosphere of those branch lines had remained through the twenty-five years of the Southern Railway, at the end of which motive power on those Sussex by-ways had mostly changed from Stroudley 'D' class 0-4-2s, to demoted Marsh express tank engines of the 'I3' 4-4-2 type.

The impending closure of the line between East Grinstead and Culver Junction, near Lewes, was announced soon after the modernization plan for British Railways had been launched — long before the days of Beeching; and the date originally fixed was 13 June 1955. But before that date there was a strike of enginemen, and the last trains actually ran on 28 May. Among the many protesters was a resident of Chailey, Miss B. E. Bessemer, who referred to original documents and found that the

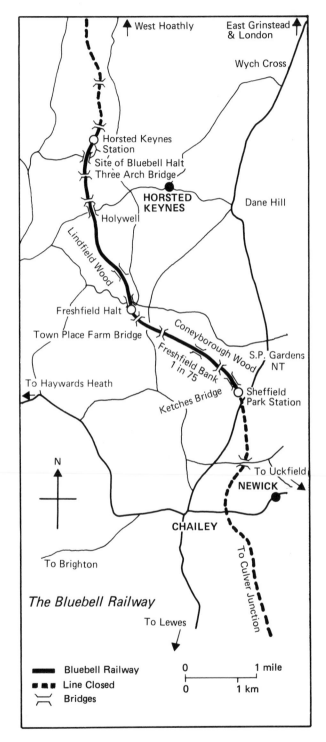

The Bluebell Railway

Bluebell Railway
Line Closed
Bridges

0   1 mile
0   1 km

railway itself could not close the line. It could only be effected by government authority. After a long wrangle, British Railways had to re-open the line, providing a minimum service of four trains per day in each direction, to comply with the Act. Re-opening took place in August 1956, and it must be admitted the B R made things as awkward as they could for passengers by refusing to issue tickets beyond the extremities of the original line. Traffic was negligible. One ex-L B S C brake-third coach sufficed for all the passengers, and financially the line was a dead loss. The case for closure was proved, but before its intended demise it had attracted a vast amount of publicity in the media and the Lewes and East Grinstead Railway Preservation Society got away to a good start.

Wittingly or unwittingly, and quite apart from any railway considerations, the society was on historic ground at each end. Nigh eighty years ago, in doing the fieldwork for his charming book *Highways and Byways in Sussex,* E. V. Lucas used the line, and explained how Horsted Keynes got its name, distinguishing it from Little Horsted, a village some miles to the east. The Keynes family can trace their ancestry back to the Norman family of de Cahanges, one of whom fought in the Battle of Hastings. The family settled in Sussex afterwards and the name became anglicized to Keynes. A railway administrative centre and mechanical engineering workshops would have been the last things associated with Sheffield Park, at the other end of the preserved line, when E. V. Lucas made his leisurely way around the county. Nearby, at the seat of the Earl of Sheffield, was one of the finest private cricket grounds in England, so spacious indeed that Australian teams visiting this country used to open their season with a match at Sheffield Park. It was not enough for the Earl to play cricket in the summer. In the very severe winter of 1890—1 they played several matches *on the ice* on one of the lakes in the park, with well-known county players on both sides!

It was the custom of the nineteenth-century Brighton railway to name engines after stations on the original line. There were 'D' class 0-4-2 tanks *Grinstead, Hoathly* and *Chailey;* Billington 0-6-2 'radial' tanks, *East Hoathly, Newick* and *Barcombe,* and a 0-4-4 tank *Horsted Keynes.* In honour of the nobleman rather than the station, however, one of the 'Gladstone' main line express engines was named *Sheffield,* though I imagine that most people who saw that engine would associate the name with the city of steel rather than with cricket on the ice in Sussex! Another association with the original line was the 0-4-2 tank engine *Brambletye,* named after an historic house near East Grinstead, and featured in a fine colour plate in Hamilton Ellis's book *Some Classic Locomotives.*

But why 'Bluebell'? There was an age-old joke, applied to many English branch lines, that the trains were so slow that the staff would willingly stop for passengers to pick flowers by the wayside; and there was the neighbouring 'Cuckoo' line to add the naturalist interest; but the name 'Bluebell' arose in quite a different way. When it was first announced that the line between East Grinstead and Culver Junction was to be closed the controversy aroused was such as to attract considerable attention in the press. Whether some of the gentlemen who journeyed thence to collect local colour found their way to West Hoathly (pronounced Ho-ly) and sought refreshment at the nearby Bluebell Inn I do not know; but in the press stories the railway was referred to as the 'Bluebell line', and the preservation society seized upon this as an inspiration, and changed their own name from the lengthy, though doubtless more accurate Lewes and East Grinstead to the Bluebell Railway Preservation Society. And so, Bluebell it has been ever since.

When the rescue operation began the line was still connected to the main Southern Region system by the branch from Copyhold Junction, through Ardingly to Horsted Keynes, which had in fact been electrified. This connection had from quite early days been used for conveying engines to a dump at Horsted Keynes for scrapping or repairs. In a photograph published in the *Railway Magazine* in December 1932 one can count no fewer than thirty engines awaiting attention of one kind or another. The date of the photograph is not stated, but a number of the engines appear to be Billinton 'radial' 0-6-2 tanks, some in the yellow livery, and many more have Stroudley copper capped chimneys.

The Bluebell line was closed to all ordinary railway traffic in March 1958, but the northern end of it, from Horsted Keynes to East Grinstead, was kept open for special workings and to provide a connection, via Ardingly, to Haywards Heath. In 1959 negotiations were in progress with the British Transport Commission for the purchase of the four and a half mile section of the line from Horsted Keynes to Sheffield Park. The price finally agreed was £34,000. To stimulate interest a 'Bluebell Special' train was run on 12 July in that year. Because of the 1958 closure it could not run over the section of line intended to be re-opened, but instead skirted the territory. Starting from Tonbridge it ran via Tunbridge Wells, East Grinstead, Horsted Keynes, Haywards Heath and Lewes to Uckfield, thence returning to Tonbridge. For the record, the train was hauled by an L B S C Marsh 0-6-0 goods engine, No. 535 (B R 32535) with top feed apparatus, giving the appearance of having two domes.

In the meantime arrangements for the re-opening were going forward, but at first the sale of the section of line southwards to Sheffield Park did not permit the Bluebell trains to enter the extensive Southern Region station at Horsted Keynes, and plans were made to erect a halt platform outside. It would make interchange between the electric service from Haywards Heath and the Bluebell line difficult, but from the outset it was expected that such difficulties would be taken in the Society's stride. The original station at Horsted Keynes is a very splendid affair, for such a deeply rural district, with the up and down tracks of the Ardingly line separate from the single-tracked Bluebell line. This latter has platform faces on both sides, the eastern side having immediate access to the lavish and handsome main station buildings. To enable the Society to operate the line a Light Railway Order had to be obtained. Colonel J. R. H. Robertson made the necessary inspection on behalf of the Ministry of Transport, and the Order was issued in July 1960.

Two months earlier, however, a memorable event had taken place at Horsted Keynes. The Society had purchased from British Railways one of the ever-famous Stroudley 0-6-0 'Terrier' tank engines. In B R stock this was No. 32655, originally No. 55 *Stepney,* built at Brighton in December 1875. She had been given a thorough overhaul at Eastleigh and arrived at Horsted Keynes smartly finished in black, lined out in red, and numbered 55. Those with an eye to true historical accuracy, so far as Bluebell line motive power was concerned, might have wished for a 'D' class 0-4-2; but to get a late Victorian Stroudley tank engine that was already nearly eighty-five years old was a very good second choice. The two carriages that arrived with it were not so attractive, and were of a completely different period from the engine. It was not long before the latter had been gorgeously repainted in Stroudley's famous 'improved engine green' — otherwise yellow ochre, with all its elaborate lining out.

The special arrangements at Horsted Keynes, where at first Bluebell trains were not to be allowed into the Southern Region station, and where the new 'station' was to consist of no more than a platform on the branch where it had become single line, meant that there would be no facilities for an engine to run round its train. The Society was given to understand that authority to operate the line would be granted only on the understanding that an engine would be provided at each end of a train. No propelling would be permitted. So, at this

Horsted Keynes—Sheffield Park train descending Freshfield bank, hauled by ex-L S W R 4-4-2T No. 488 and ex-S E & C R 0-6-0 No. 592, May 1975

Brian Morrison

early stage the Society had to look round for a second engine. They found one in the shape of a tiny little 'P' class 0-6-0 tank of the former S E & C R, the Ashford counterpart of the Brighton 'Terrier', though built thirty-five years later, old No. 323. These engines, of which no more than eight were built, were originally rather feeble little things barely strong enough for the light branch and push-pull work they were designed to do; and although they lasted a long time they had, for very many years, been relegated to yard and pilot work.

The comparison with the Stroudley Terriers is interesting.

Railway	Cylinders dia.	stroke	Coupled wheel dia. ft-in.	Boiler pressure psi
L B & S C R	13	20	4-0	140
S E & C R	12	18	3-9	160

Even when originally built, with thirteen-inch cylinders the Brighton engines had a greater tractive effort; but when this dimension was enlarged to fourteen inches the disparity became considerably greater, to a 25 per cent advantage. Nevertheless, smartly turned out and named Bluebell, it made a pretty sight, and with *Stepney* at one end and *Bluebell* at the other the inaugural train on 7 August 1960 set the rejuvenated railway off to an excellent start.

This inaugural train was something of an improbable mix-up, with a Brighton engine at one end and a South Eastern and Chatham at the

At Horsted Keynes, the American-type 0-6-0T No. 30064, built by Vulcan Foundry Ltd, 1943. In the right foreground a fine example of an L B & S C R type of semaphore signal, July 1973 *David Eatwell*

24

other, and between them an early Southern corridor brake-third, and a lengthened L S W R coach on a Southern underframe. Historically such an assemblage was a non-starter. But such had been the publicity surrounding the initial threat to close the railway and its re-opening that the public flocked to see it in operation again. By the time the line closed for the winter on 30 October some 15,000 passengers had been carried in those two coaches, pulled and pushed by those little 0-6-0 tank engines. The sociologists might find it difficult to explain why so many people found it such an attraction. No one went out of his way to travel on these rural branch lines when they were operating normally. Railway enthusiasts visited some of them, and wrote learned articles in the technical press; but of general interest, and above all interest that brought the whole family for a day out, there was virtually none. I think it is a natural British reaction when something that has been an institution, a neglected and little noticed institution, is threatened with removal. The news media, in all its forms, ready enough to castigate the railways on the very slightest provocation, became ready to champion those who rose in opposition.

At all events, the Bluebell line got away to a magnificent start, and during the winter of 1960—1 there was time to prepare for a much longer season, and, it was hoped, many more passengers. But with only two locomotives, both old — one very old! — and both required for every train, the line would be operating on a shoestring. More locomotives and more carriages were required, and as it was not found possible to get another 'Terrier' from B R, a second ex-S E & C R 'P' class 0-6-0 was obtained. At about the same time, and in readiness for the 1961 season, four ex-Metropolitan coaches were purchased. These had been made redundant by the electrification of the Chesham line, and during the summer of 1961 two more locomotives of great historical interest were added to the stock. These were an ex-London and South Western 'radial' 4-4-2 tank of William Adams's design, which from 1919 had been working on the East Kent Railway, and an ex-North London Railway outside-cylindered 0-6-0 tank engine.

It will be appreciated from this that the Bluebell line was gathering its working stock without any particular regard to its having any connection with the original operation of the line, either in L B S C or in Southern days. This brought some criticism from the purists, particularly when the ex-S E & C R 0-6-0 tank engines were named, in the Stroudley style in large letters on their side tanks, *Bluebell* and *Primrose*. The management had, however, to think of popular appeal; and although the railway's first engine, the Brighton 'Terrier' No. 55, had her original name added when she was restored to the yellow livery and looked a glorious little period piece, true in all respects to the locale, visitors to the bookstall on Sheffield Park station bought twelve postcards of *Bluebell* to every one of *Stepney!* This endorsed the policy of the Society to acquire vintage locomotives and coaching stock when and where they were available, and when they could be afforded!

The 1961 season exceeded all expectations, not only in the thousands of visitors who came to the line but in the demands made upon it for film and television documentaries, and as the scene for films that needed an old-time railway as setting for some of the episodes. British Railways, observing that the Bluebell line was being run in a thoroughly professional manner, were being much more co-operative; at the end of October 1961 the embargo at Horsted Keynes was removed, and the first Bluebell train, hauled and pushed by four locomotives, entered the Southern Region station, using the platform with faces on both sides of the track. In 1962 through excursion trains to Sheffield Park began running, and in a notable case from London (Victoria) worked by an ex-L S W R 4-4-0 of the 'T9' class, engines of the Bluebell Railway took over the haulage at Haywards Heath. There the train had to reverse direction, and the preserved engines hauled the special over the Southern Region branch to Horsted Keynes.

The physical connection with British Railways

at Horsted Keynes seemed invaluable for this developing business. The Bluebell Railway was extending its facilities at Sheffield Park to build up an operational museum of historic locomotives and stock, irrespective of whether they had any association with the old line; and the connecting line from Horsted Keynes to Copyhold Junction on the Brighton main line was the link over which new acquisitions came. A new arrival in the winter of 1961–2 was an ex-Great Western 'Duke-dog' 4-4-0, No. 9017. This had previously been lying in store at Oswestry, and had been rescued by a private preservation fund, before being handed over to the Bluebell line. The engine was subsequently restored to Great Western livery and given its original number 3217. Furthermore it then received the name *Earl of Berkeley* which had been intended for it, but which it had never carried on the G W R. The story is well known that engines of the '32XX' class had been completed at Swindon in 1937 up to 3212, all carrying the names of Earls, and that then suddenly, before any more were turned out, the names on Nos 3200–12 were removed, and all the class thenceforward ran nameless. The eminent gentlemen after whom these engines were being named apparently objected to being represented on such relatively unimportant engines, and arrangements were made for an equivalent number of 'Castle' class 4-6-0s to be renamed in their honour.

By the time the *Earl of Berkeley* (alias 9017) arrived, the Beeching investigations were in full blast, and there was consternation among some supporters of the Bluebell Railway when it was known that the B R link from Haywards Heath to Horsted Keynes was on the condemned list, even though it was electrified. The preserved line would then be completely isolated, out in the Sussex countryside 'beginning nowhere and leading to nowhere', as was once said of another railway in the hectic promotion days of the nineteenth century. But so far as the Bluebell Railway was concerned the severing of the B R link, which took place on 28 October 1963 made little or no difference. Enthusiasts of all ages and both sexes

flocked to see it in their cars, or travelling to Haywards Heath, and thence by the connecting bus service. But the most remarkable thing of all was that the Bluebell line continued to accumulate what were becoming vintage locomotives, and very interesting items of coaching stock, even though they had to make the last stage of the journey to Sheffield Park by road. In view of these acquisitions, many of which are privately owned and lodged with the Bluebell for safe keeping, many people have questioned whether it would not have paid to purchase the condemned connecting link; but the occasional cost of hiring a low-loader to bring an engine or carriage to Sheffield Park is negligible compared to the cost of maintaining a length of railway almost equal to that already in hand.

And so, with the passing of the years, this first of the new private railways prospered, and the present tally of rolling stock is 24 steam locomotives, 2 petrol-driven locomotives, 37 passenger carriages and 10 freight wagons. The majority of the locomotives are from the Southern, and its pre-grouping constituents. The South Eastern and Chatham is particularly well represented, because in addition to the two little 'P' class 0-6-0 tanks, there is a Wainwright class 'C' 0-6-0 goods, and one of the splendid 'H' class 0-4-4 suburban tanks — both these latter in the full glory of the Wainwright livery. Representing the Brighton in addition to the two little 'Terriers' is the 0-6-2 radial tank *Birch Grove*, showing to perfection the Marsh dark umber livery, while the Adams 4-4-2 tank admirably keeps the memory of the nineteenth-century South Western freshly in mind. The management can be commended for its catholicity of taste in locomotives; but while such a large and really incongruous addition, on a rural branch line, as a Bulleid 'West Country' Pacific was undoubtedly an attraction, I think the line

Sheffield Park station, ex-S E & C R 0-4-4T No. 263 (built 1905) ready to leave for Horsted Keynes, December 1978
David Eatwell

At Horsted Keynes the ex-L S W R 4-4-2T No. 488 (built 1885) with the ex-Great Northern Directors' saloon, December 1975   *David Eatwell*

should have been drawn at giving 'house room', even temporarily, to such an unspeakable horror as the Bulleid 'Q1' class 0-6-0. I am aware that in wartime there may have been a case for dragging British locomotive design to such depths; but once their usefulness was ended the nearest refuse dump would seem to be more appropriate for these engines than a place in a museum!

There are always likely to be differences of opinion, or of taste, when it comes to the preservation of railway relics, but there can be little cause for disagreement over some of the beautiful period carriages that have come to the Bluebell Railway. There is a very handsome teak-bodied Great Northern clerestory-roofed saloon dating back to 1897, among the earliest of the large bogie vehicles used on that railway; and for me, a vehicle with the happiest of nostalgic memories, a London and North Western observation car in

which I rode sixty years ago, on the rear of one of the regular branch line trains from Llandudno Junction up the Conway Valley to Bettws-y-coed, and then through the long tunnel to Blaenau Festiniog. It is a lovely vehicle to have on the Bluebell Railway especially now that it has been restored to the L N W R livery. All in all, the Bluebell Railway, by its initial success and its continued interest and excellence of display has set a pattern and laid a foundation for a new era in British steam railways. It is interesting to follow how the formula for rescue operations has been worked out in many different areas, each with its own historical background.

3

Kent And East Sussex

In August 1896 Parliament passed the Light Railways Act to facilitate principally in Ireland the construction of light, and if necessary substandard gauge lines in rural districts. The intention was to provide relatively cheap transport on railways where speed was to be limited to 25 mph and on which the constructional work could be lighter and less expensive than on an ordinary railway. The Act appointed three Light Railway Commissioners, and application for an Order to authorize a light railway had to be made to the Commissioners. It was not necessary to obtain an Act of Parliament. The Commissioners could only recommend, and an application had no effect until confirmed by the Board of Trade. When an Order had been confirmed, however, it had all the legal force of an Act of Parliament.

In this interesting period in British railway history a young engineer, Holman Fred Stephens, had just completed his training in the locomotive department of the Metropolitan Railway at Neasden, and one of his first jobs was to act as Resident Engineer for the construction of the Cranbrook and Paddock Wood branch of the South Eastern Railway. This of course had to be built to main line standards, and the expense of construction on a line that could not be expected to have a heavy traffic was no doubt brought home to him. When in 1896 the Rother Valley Railway,

only a few miles away, was authorized under the Light Railways Act, he not only became its managing director, engineer, and locomotive superintendent but espoused the cause of light railways generally. The Rother Valley was actually the very first to be authorized under the Act; in this respect it created an unusual amount of interest, and although not opened until 2 April 1900 it was the subject of an illustrated article in the *Railway Magazine* only three months later. The author was Victor L. Whitechurch, a frequent and entertaining contributor in those early years of the magazine, but he slipped up at the finish in expressing his thanks for a ride on the footplate to Mr H. F. Stephen*son!* The section originally opened ran from its junction with the Hastings line of the South Eastern and Chatham, at Robertsbridge, to a station at first called Tenterden, but which was actually at the foot of the hill on which that charming little town is built. It thus avoided the 1 in 50 gradient that was necessary when the line was extended. The original Tenterden station was then named Rolvenden.

When first opened the line was twelve and a quarter miles long, and had two locomotives, six four-wheeled passenger carriages, two brake vans, and ten trucks, and to operate a service of six passenger trains a day in each direction the total staff consisted of one platelayer per mile, two

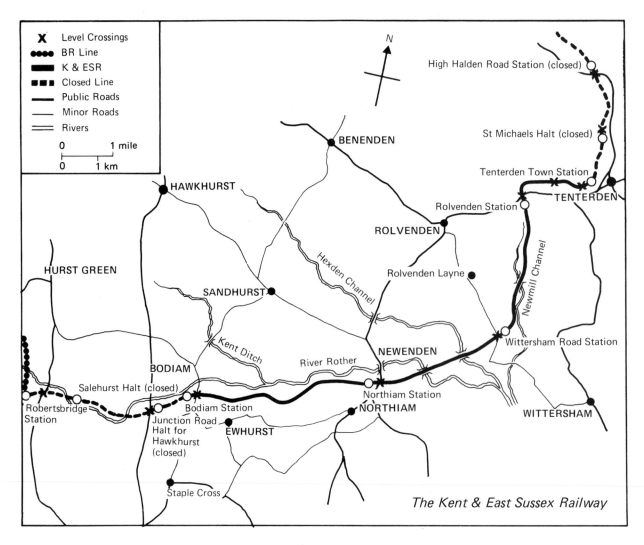

The Kent & East Sussex Railway

station men at Northiam and Tenterden, two station lads at Bodiam and Wittersham Road, two engine drivers, two cleaners, two guards, one gate man and one gate woman. In that article in the *Railway Magazine* it was reported that the running costs were working out at one shilling per train mile. There were no ticket offices at the stations. The Rother Valley introduced the prototype of the modern pay-train, with the guard walking through the train and issuing tickets on the journey. At the outset all the equipment was new. The two locomotives, built by R. & W.

Hawthorn, Leslie & Co. of Newcastle, were little outside-cylindered 2-4-0s weighing no more than twenty-four tons, and named *Northiam* and *Tenterden*. They were painted dark blue, lined out in red, in a style that Whitechurch likened to that of the Great Eastern Railway. The four-wheeled coaches, in polished teak, were built by Hurst, Nelson & Co. of Motherwell. The Rother Valley was not only the first of Stephens's railways, but was unique in having everything new at the start, whereas his later railways had to make do with second- or third-hand rolling stock.

The track was laid with flat-bottomed rails weighing 60 lb per yard, and the fresh and substantial ballasting evident in early photographs looks distinctly better than that of the South Eastern and Chatham line where they adjoin at Robertsbridge. At the outset the Board of Trade imposed a speed limit of 15 mph, though this was subsequently raised to the statutory 25 mph maximum for a 'light railway'. The line was single throughout, with one passing loop at Northiam station, roughly half way between Tenterden and Robertsbridge. The staff and ticket system of single line working was used, but except at Robertsbridge, where there was physical connection with the S E & C R line, there were no signal cabins. The few signals at Tenterden and Northiam passing loop were actuated from ground frames. It was altogether a very smart little railway, and evidently most economically run.

From the very outset it was clear that Stephens regarded the Rother Valley line as a mere beginning, and he pressed ahead and secured authorization for three extensions: one climbed from Rolvenden into Tenterden Town, and a mile further on turned sharply to the west to continue through hilly country to make a junction with the branch he had built for the South Eastern at Cranbrook; a second ran from Northiam down to Rye, while the third and most ambitious of all ran from Robertsbridge to a junction with the L B & S C R at Pevensey. In the event none of these was built, but authorization was obtained for a line northward from Tenterden to link up with the South Eastern main line at Headcorn, and this line was opened in 1905. This was the ultimate extent of the line, and it was at that time that the name was changed to the Kent & East Sussex Railway. It was undisturbed by grouping in 1923, and it was not until 1948 that there was any change; and then it became part of British Railways. But I must go back to the year 1905, when the K & E S R attained its maximum route mileage of twenty-one and a half, and consolidated the character that endeared it to all its patrons and friends.

In those halcyon days before World War I the expectations surrounding this modest little railway must have been considerable. As a means of public transport the internal combustion engine was an unknown quantity, and here was a light railway, with nicely appointed, brand new coaching stock, working through one of the loveliest and most unspoiled regions of England. Books of topographical interest, such as the *Highways and Byways* series from Macmillan & Co., or the sumptuously illustrated colour books from Adam & Charles Black with whom I myself have had very happy relations, were awakening new interest in the countryside, and when

Page from South-Eastern and Chatham Railway Official Guide

distinguished authors did not hesitate to use leisurely lines of railway to reach newly noticed beauty spots those who followed in their footsteps were ready enough to do likewise.

The little light railway was certainly well publicized in the South Eastern and Chatham Railway Official Guide, and on its system map shown as prominently as any of its own branch lines. The write-up, interposed in the description of the Hastings line, was somewhat euphemistic:

The little village of Robertsbridge, which lies to the left of the main line to Hastings and on the banks of the Rother, was in bygone days chiefly known for its pleasantly situated Cistercian abbey, a foundation of the twelfth century, of which nought remains save a few fragmentary ruins. But it has recently become a station of some importance, by reason of its connection with the trains of the Kent and East Sussex Light Railway *which run hence through a picturesque countryside to the market town of Tenterden. Certain stations on the line are conveniently situated for the fishing reaches of the Rother. The Company's trains, comprising first and third class carriages, depart after the arrival of the London express . . .*

Those chatty little remarks did not, however, tell you how long it took to cover the remaining thirteen and a half miles to Tenterden Town. I do not know what the connections were like prior to 1914, but in 1938 the 9.30 a.m. from Charing Cross arrived at Robertsbridge at 10.54, and although the K & E S R train left at 11.15, it did not stagger into Tenterden until 12.25 p.m. The afternoon train was faster, and covered the thirteen and a half miles in 40 minutes. I cannot recall that the line ever featured in *British Locomotive Practice and Performance*. The line had a full-page advertisement in the South Eastern and Chatham Railway Official Guide, which is reproduced on page 31; and certainly Bodiam Castle, so prominently featured, and which can be seen to the north of the line near Bodiam station, is one of the 'lions' of topography in the district. This magnificent moated stronghold was built in 1386,

and at that time seagoing ships could penetrate the Rother as far as Bodiam. The remains of the small harbour can still be seen.

The regular traffic that developed in the early days was not very heavy, but the line ran through one of the finest hop growing areas in Kent. In the summer season hordes of hop pickers used to descend upon the railway and special trains had to be run. They do not go any more, but the tiny huts provided for them are still to be seen. The hop-pickers' specials, like many another sharply seasonal traffic, were an embarrassment in some respects, because they involved the keeping in readiness rolling stock that was very much under-utilized for the rest of the year. Nevertheless the business was profitable enough while it lasted, and had to be provided for.

When it came to augmenting the locomotive stock Stephens turned to the very-willing Stroudley Terriers, and engine No. 70 of the L B & S C R, named *Poplar*, and already twenty-nine years old, was purchased in 1901. It became K & E S R and was named *Bodiam*. As might be expected, it proved ideal for the job, more powerful than the Hawthorn 2-4-0s, and a second engine of the same type was added in 1905. This was L B S C No. 671 *Wapping*, which became No. 5 and was appropriately named *Rolvenden*.

In readiness for the northward extension to Headcorn three new trains composed entirely of bogie stock were purchased from R. Y. Pickering & Co. They each consisted of three coaches: a brake-composite, a third, and a brake-third. However, the severe gradients of the northward extension gave some concern when freight was carried. Although the Company had little capacity for carrying traffic within its own system, a considerable volume came to be handed over by the S E & C R at both ends. It was for this that Mr Stephens designed a powerful 0-8-0 tank engine, which was built by Hawthorn, Leslie & Co. in 1904.

This neat and handsomely styled locomotive No. 4, *Hecate*, had cylinders 16 in. diameter by 24 in. stroke, and coupled wheels 4 ft 3 in. diameter. The cylinders which were outside drove on to the third pair of wheels, and to facilitate the negotiation of the sharp curves on the line the driving wheels were flangeless. The wheels were closely spaced, and the wheelbase was only 15 ft 4 in. The total weight of the engine in working was 43½ tons. The engine was very smartly finished in dark blue, with red lining, and a copper top to the chimney, polished brass dome, and safety valve casing. I have seen it suggested that this fine engine was not entirely a success, and that on account of its weight it could not be used on the original section of the line between Rolvenden and Robertsbridge; but she remained on the line until 1932 when she was exchanged with the Southern Railway for a Beattie 0-6-0 saddle tank of 1876 vintage.

Prior to this Mr Stephens had maintained his more usual policy of obtaining suitable rolling stock second hand, and before World War I two 0-6-0 tender engines had been purchased from the London and South Western Railway, these being of the so-called 'Ilfracombe Goods' class, built by Beyer, Peacock & Co. in 1873. They became No. 7, *Rother,* and No. 9, *Juno,* on the K & E S R. But in the difficult year after the end of the war the line, which had never paid a dividend of more than 3 per cent, and often much less, was left out in the wilderness. Had it been absorbed into the Southern at the time of grouping its working might have been integrated to some extent with the adjoining lines, and the inevitable losses on its traffic borne by other areas that were more profitable. But with the rapid increase in road transport and of motor omnibus services a light railway like the K & E S R stood no chance.

Stephens, now Lieut.-Colonel after his war service in the Royal Engineers, was in failing health and in 1931 he died. Shortly afterwards the railway went into liquidation, and the business was carried on by the Receiver, W. H. Austen, who took over the offices of General Manager and Engineer. He had been assistant to Colonel Stephens, and in difficult circumstances he managed to operate the railway for a further sixteen years. It was not to be expected that with such a financial incubus hanging over the line, with

first of all the great depression and then war conditions, that much could have been done to keep the line and its equipment up to date. It was indeed to the immense credit of all concerned that it was kept going at all. Then, on New Year's Day 1948, in company with all the standard gauge railways of Britain, great and small, it was nationalized, and became part of the new Southern Region. One might have imagined that the new overlords would have taken one look at it and marked it down for early closure, but they came in and completely relaid the track from end to end. The early flat-bottomed rails had long since been replaced by bull-head track which Stephens had no doubt obtained at a knock-down second- or third-hand price; but this in turn was now completely renewed.

Although continued austerity in the post-war years, and petrol rationing, limited the amount of competition from alternative sources of transport, traffic on the line became less and less, and even before the modernization plan for British Railways was launched, and Beeching was a name unknown except in the chemical industry, regular services on the K & E S line of Southern Region were withdrawn as from 2 January 1954. Furthermore, the track between Tenterden Town and Headcorn was summarily lifted. Prior to this, business had dwindled to such an extent that on the older section, to Robertsbridge, a typical train had consisted of one coach and a few wagons, hauled, inevitably, by a gallant little 'Terrier' tank engine. After the withdrawal of regular passenger services, in 1954, it was extraordinary that the line managed to keep going at all, in view of the hardening official attitude towards unproductive and insolvent sections of line. In the summer months there were occasional hop pickers' specials, and freight trains of a kind were run, hauled, unromantically, by 204 hp 0-6-0 diesel mechanical locomotives. These ceased on 12 July 1961.

By that time the sparsely used little line was nevertheless held in so much regard and affection that a determined effort was started up immediately for its preservation. No later than 15 July 1961 the first Annual General Meeting of the Kent and East Sussex Railway Preservation Society was held in the Town Hall of Tenterden. The enthusiasts of the Bluebell Railway had shown what could be done, though the very nearness of the latter enterprise posed a few problems for the K & E S R. Would support for a second light railway be so readily forthcoming? In fact the Kent and East Sussex was of far greater historical interest than the Bluebell. While the latter, for all its charm, was no more than part of a branch line of the Brighton railway, the K & E S R was not only the very first in the United Kingdom to be built under the provisions of the Light Railway Act, 1896, but it was particularly associated with the colourful personality of Colonel Stephens.

It is nevertheless difficult at times to balance outstanding historical interest against legal problems, and the availability, or otherwise, of hard cash; and for a very anxious ten years preservationists had a rough ride. Then, in 1971, the Tenterden Railway Company was formed and plans made to restore ten miles of line between Tenterden and Bodiam.

Ten years of dereliction! No gardener needs to be told what ten *weeks* of inaction on his part can do to a hitherto trim garden; but imagine what can happen in ten *years* in a lush and very fertile countryside where weeds and saplings grow with riotous abandon unless checked. In those ten miles of one-time railway between Tenterden and Bodiam much of the track was completely hidden, while elsewhere growth of the young trees on either side had led the branches to meet in the middle of what had been the railway right of way. This was no place for faint hearts among the preservationists, and having cleared away ten years' growth there was the small matter of re-opening twenty miles of ditches to ensure proper drainage of the track.

The Kent and East Sussex Railway was successful in securing financial aid from the Manpower Services Commission in the form of grants under the Job Creation Programme for the employment of young people in the rehabilitation of the line and its buildings. Up to forty unskilled persons have been employed at a time, under suitable supervision, for work on the track, installation of new sidings, and building locomotive and carriage repair shops. That this labour has been very effectively used is evident; but the actual running of the railway, which is approximately the same length as the Bluebell line, is almost entirely in the hands of volunteers.

Once again it was a case of a light railway 'out in the midst of nowhere', although of course Tenterden is very much 'somewhere'; nevertheless it was a railway whose every connection with the main line network of Great Britain had been severed. That did not prevent a remarkable collection of locomotives and stock being gathered there. By 1980 I should think the new Kent and East Sussex Railway, operated by the Tenterden Railway Co. Ltd, had the most unusual tally of equipment of any railway in the world, in that locomotives outnumbered coaching stock by two to one, 24 to 12. True the company also had 16 of what were termed departmental vehicles; but these were in no way available for conveying passengers. The re-opening in February 1974 was of no more than four miles of line westwards from Tenterden Town, yet it included the quite extensive yards at Rolvenden, where the 20 steam locomotives, 3 diesels, and one diesel railcar were kept. It was of course much more of a museum than a motive power depot adequate to run the modest existing traffic of the re-opened railway; but such a varied assemblage of steam locomotives, smartly refurbished and in working condition, has been as great an attraction in itself as having a ride on one of the trains.

It is perhaps a coincidence that two of the most historic locomotive classes represented on the line

Ex-L B & S C R Stroudley 'Terrier' 0-6-0T No. 10 *Sutton* propelling train up the gradient towards Tenterden, April 1979   *Brian Morrison*

One of the Hunslet 'Austerity' 0-6-0T locomotives No. 23 climbing the bank into Tenterden with an eastbound train, September 1976   *Brian Morrison*

are 0-6-0 tanks, though of very different origin and vintage — the Stroudley 'Terriers' and the Hunslet 'Austerities' of World War II. Each in its turn proved to be a remarkably tough and versatile workhorse, though it is doubtful if the Hunslets will achieve the longevity of the Stroudleys. In 1942, to back up the armies that were being gradually built up in the United Kingdom for re-entry to the European Continent, large numbers of locomotives were needed — a main line type and a heavy shunter. The Minister of Supply made it clear to representatives of the locomotive industry that he wanted two years of hard intensive work from these locomotives, but after that he did not much care what happened to them. There was no time, materials or money for refinements in design, and so far as the shunter was concerned the Hunslet 'Austerity' 0-6-0 tank was the result. It proved outstandingly successful. Hunslet drawings were passed to other manufacturers, and they augmented the stock, while after the war the National Coal Board ordered forty in 1952 to become the standard colliery shunter of the post-war world. Several are now in the service of the K & E S R and it was a very happy gesture on behalf of the present management to name one of them *Holman F. Stephens,* in a ceremony at Tenterden on 14 May 1977, at which the Keeper of the National Railway Museum, Dr John Coiley, was present.

The Stroudley 'Terrier' 0-6-0 tanks seem to be ageless! No. 3 *Bodiam,* originally No. 70 *Poplar* of the L B & S C R, which was built in 1872, is probably the oldest standard gauge locomotive in service in the country, while her sister now No. 10 *Sutton* is only three years her junior. The latter came to the K & E S R as British Railways, No. 32650, unnamed; and in restoring her original name the new owners have, unconsciously perhaps, recalled a characteristically amusing passage in one of the late E. L. Ahrons's articles in the *Railway Magazine* of more than sixty years ago. Referring to the nineteenth-century practice of the 'Brighton' railway of naming engines after stations and villages on the line, and the unsuitability and often faintly humorous nature of some of the names, he continued: 'besides, too, it was sometimes a source of confusion to old ladies, who, on discovering a string of carriages at Victoria with an engine at the back, the latter being labelled *Sutton* in large gilt letters on the side tanks — this being just the very station they wanted — sampled the train and duly found themselves in the Peckham Rye country or at some other equally interesting spot where they did not want to be landed'.

The centenary of *Sutton* was celebrated by a 'Grand Steam Weekend' on 25/26 September 1976 during which a cavalcade of nine locomotives was staged. At that time this beautiful little engine was nearly 101 years old, on the authority of the *Locomotive Magazine* of August 1898, and in leading the cavalcade away from Tenterden she hauled a most unusual vehicle for a light railway: nothing less than one of the diesel-mechanical express railcars of the Great Western Railway. On this gala occasion on the K & E S R the car was not working under its own power, but was being used to provide additional seating accommodation. I have vivid recollections of some very fast running in one of these cars on an express duty west of Carmarthen in 1947, in which we several times ran at 70 mph and a little over.

The Stroudley 'Terrier' 0-6-0T No. 10 *Sutton* at
Tenterden, September 1976   *Brian Morrison*

In 1967 I had the pleasure of reviewing for the *Engineer* a splendid book, written by a Norfolkman and published by a Norfolk firm, entitled *A Short History of the Midland and Great Northern Joint Railway*. This line had a chequered, varied and latterly distinguished history until nationalization came in 1948, and turned the whole railway situation in Norfolk topsy-turvy. That it continued as a joint line through the twenty-five years of grouping, though welcome enough to all who knew it and worked on it, was something of an indictment of the way the amalgamations were arranged in 1923. The new groupings were made according to the territories owned by the old companies and not in a rational geographical manner so that a line that had been jointly owned by the Midland and Great Northern became equally joint between the L M S and the L N E R. Its main line running from an end-on junction with the Midland Railway at Bourne, via South Lynn, Sutton Bridge and Melton Constable measured no less than 107½ miles to Yarmouth, and 120 if one went on to Lowestoft.

Today it is little more than a memory, but a memory enthusiastically honoured by the members of the Midland and Great Northern Joint Railway Society Limited, founded in 1959 to try and preserve as a working unit some section of the old railway. Like all the railways discussed in this book the M & G N Joint had a history that makes fascinating reading today, and which in many ways was unique in the humble, disjointed origins that were eventually linked up to make an important main line system. For make no mistake about it, the M & G N Joint was a main trunk line of considerable importance. It was not until 1883 that its predecessor, the Eastern and Midlands Railway, began to take some co-ordinated form, when a number of small local railways in Norfolk were amalgamated. Ahrons describes them picturesquely: '... some of which apparently began in a field at the back of nowhere and ended in another field a long way from anywhere else'. How these bits and pieces of railway became linked together to form the main line through to Yarmouth, with branches north and south from its nodal point of Melton Constable to Cromer on the one side and Norwich on the other, is really beside the point, except perhaps to mention, as Ahrons recalls, that if you searched for Melton Constable in a Bradshaw of 1880 you would not find it, for the simple reason that railway-wise it did not then exist.

In 1883, the year of the amalgamation that set up the Eastern and Midlands Railway, the company was fortunate in securing the services of a young engineer, then no more than twenty-six years of age, who became to the railway and its

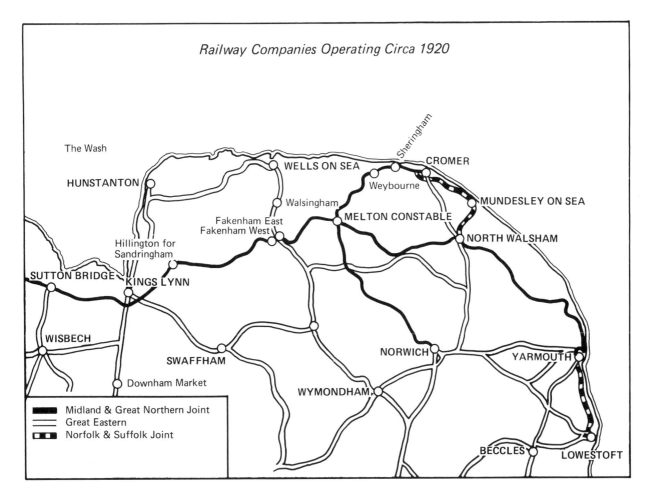

Railway Companies Operating Circa 1920

The Wash
HUNSTANTON
WELLS ON SEA
Sheringham
CROMER
Weybourne
Walsingham
MELTON CONSTABLE
MUNDESLEY ON SEA
Fakenham East
Fakenham West
NORTH WALSHAM
Hillington for Sandringham
SUTTON BRIDGE
KINGS LYNN
WISBECH
SWAFFHAM
NORWICH
YARMOUTH
Downham Market
WYMONDHAM
Midland & Great Northern Joint
Great Eastern
Norfolk & Suffolk Joint
BECCLES
LOWESTOFT

'Joint Line' successor as great a 'father figure' as Holman Stephens became in his 'light railway' sphere. This was William Marriott, who had served a pupilage with Messrs Ransome & Rapier, the famous Ipswich firm of engineers. His career thereafter was entirely in East Anglia. His original appointment was that of Engineer, but he also acted as Locomotive Superintendent, and under the later joint ownership he was resident manager. There is no doubt that the 'wise men' of the Midland and the Great Northern realized they had in him a first class man, a local man in tune with all the local requirements both of engineering and train service, and were glad enough for him to carry on. And carry on he did, for forty-one years.

The Joint Line became a veritable monument to his all-round ability as an engineer and as a railwayman. In due course he became a pioneer in the use of reinforced concrete for a great variety of railway structures.

Melton Constable was almost entirely of his creation, but even in the greatest days of the railway it never grew to be more than a large village. The site was chosen and construction started by the largest of the constituents of the Eastern and Midlands, the Lynn and Fakenham, under the enthusiastic patronage of Lord Hastings, the principal landowner. In 1881, when the work was started, the population was 118, and twenty years later it had not increased to much over 900. The principal factor in the creation and development of Melton Constable as a railway and engineering centre was that it was an entirely indigenous growth, staffed by men born and bred in the Norfolk countryside, and having all that pride, independence, and almost insularity of outlook that is characteristic of the county itself. How wise were the joint owners from 1893 in not attempting to impose alien ideas, however good they might have been.

Marriott, apparently at the suggestion of his wife, painted his engines a rich yellow, the colour of the golden gorse that adorns the Norfolk country-side each summer. He had a quaint lot to look after when he became Locomotive Superintendent in 1884. It had been agreed, on the amalgamation a year earlier, that the Midland Railway should exercise a degree of supervision over the locomotive department, and in the same year that he took over Marriott received from Sharp, Stewart & Co. a batch of twenty-six splendid 4-4-0 passenger engines of the Johnson 6 ft 6 in. design, that was already doing excellent work on many parts of the Midland Railway. The artistic lines and flowing curves of these beautiful engines never looked better than when set off by Marriott's 'golden gorse' livery with the Joint Line's handsome coat of arms on the leading splasher. All engines of the batch were delivered to Derby, and 'run in' on local trains from there, but after that it was a case of 'over to you'. These engines were maintained entirely from the works at Melton Constable. There was no interference from Derby and it was a source of amusement and gratification to Joint Line enginemen, when they took over heavy holiday expresses from the Midland at Bourne, that while the expresses were frequently brought in by two Midland engines, the Joint Line men would not think of taking an assistant engine themselves. The Midland might have quite strict load limits for each class of engine, but they did not apply or were quietly disregarded east of Bourne.

It was this pride in their own railway that made Norfolk railwaymen so angry after nationaliza-tion, when it was clear that traffic was being diverted from their line. This insidious procedure had begun even before World War II, but the war itself found the Joint Line serving no fewer than ten major aerodromes, and the period of austerity afterwards, with paid holidays and the con-tinuance of petrol rationing, led to unprecedented holiday traffic from the Midlands to East Anglia, with many extra trains at weekends. But before the final closure took place in 1959, considerable changes in the working of the Joint had occurred when the responsibility for the locomotive depart-ment had been transferred from the L M S to the L N E R in 1936. After nationalization the Eastern Region of British Railways had the job of provid-ing the motive power and of running the trains. Until then there had been no augmentation of motive power since the introduction of the Johnson 4-4-0s of Midland design. They had, in due course, been modestly upgraded, as had their counterparts on the parent system, but the provision of a larger boiler only brought them up to class '2' capacity, and in any case, despite the careful maintenance in the Melton works the frames and running gear were ageing.

Before leaving the Midland era in M & G N motive power with its golden-yellow locomotives I must refer to Marriott's own designs of locomotive. The first was a sturdy little outside-cylindered 0-6-0 shunter, though with typical Midland boiler mountings. The first was built at Melton in 1897, and others were added as required, to replace the older nondescript engines with which the various constituents of the Eastern and Midlands had opened for business. These 0-6-0s continued to be built until 1907, by which time there were nine in service. But the engines with which Marriott really caught the eye of the connoisseurs of locomotive design were his three 4-4-2 passenger tank engines for local runs. The first of them, built in 1904, was put on to the line from Yarmouth to Lowestoft, opened in the year before. They were handsomely proportioned, if not very powerful locomotives, and although an indigenous M & G N product, the various fittings followed current Midland practice of the Deeley era, with a round-topped dome, Ramsbottom safety valves and a chimney that tapered outwards slightly from the base. They certainly caught the eye of the railway publicists, and the Locomotive Publishing Company had two different pictures of them in the famous F. Moore series of coloured picture postcards. These pictures show them in the original form, with the tops of their large side tanks horizontal from back to front. These may have somewhat obstructed the look-out ahead when drawing up to couple on to a train, prior to making a bunker-first trip, because at a later date the tanks were cut to have the top surface sloping down towards the front. For the record, they had 17½ in. by 24 in. cylinders, coupled wheels 6 ft 0 in. diameter, and carried a boiler pressure of 160 lb per sq. in. The remaining two engines of the class were built in 1909.

The heights of prestige for the Joint Line locomotives were reached in the early 1900s in the working of the daily through express between Norwich and Leicester. On these the earlier practice of changing from an M & G N to a Midland engine (or engines!) at Bourne was waived, and one of Marriott's rebuilt 4-4-0s, with the larger Midland class '2' boiler and Belpaire firebox worked right through. It was a lengthy run, of 124 miles, and over a difficult road, taking about four hours. The M & G N engines involved were stationed at Norwich and worked the train on alternate days, with the men lodging overnight at Leicester. At Melton Constable it collected through carriages from Cromer, Yarmouth and Lowestoft. It was a matter of pride with the M & G N men that the engines working those turns were absolutely spotless. This one through express running all the year round was something analogous to the 'Pines Express' over the Somerset and Dorset Joint Railway, between Bournemouth and Bath, with connections northward to cities of the Midlands and Lancashire. Its M & G N counterpart originated at Birmingham, though in East Anglia it was always known as the 'Leicester', because that was as far as the Joint Line locomotive worked.

Between the two world wars the working on the M & G N was changed, and the main train went to Yarmouth, providing a connection to Norwich by through carriage, and the through locomotive working became even longer, 144¾ miles. At last we are getting near to the 'Joint Line' of today, because a section of the coastal route from Yarmouth is now preserved. In the 1930s the Cromer and Yarmouth sections of the 'Leicester' express ran separately to Melton Constable, there to be joined also to the portion from Norwich. The Yarmouth section did not take the coastal route but went direct from North Walsham to Melton, via Aylsham. When the almost complete closure of the entire M & G N system took place in February 1959 an attempt was at first made to form a preservation society to save the section of line between North Walsham and Yarmouth Beach, nearly twenty-five miles of line, but this was soon seen to be a far greater job than could be undertaken, and it was not until the summer of 1965 that a definite preservation project began to get off the ground. Then the M & G N Joint Railway Society was able to purchase the section of line between Sheringham and Weybourne. It had been hoped to purchase the whole line between Sheringham and Melton Constable, eleven and a quarter miles, but insufficient money was forthcoming.

And so the 'North Norfolk Railway' was launched. By that time, unfortunately, no locomotives of the M & G N Joint Line remained; in fact there were very few locomotives left that had worked in East Anglia in pre-nationalization days. It might indeed seem that nemesis had overtaken the Joint Line, when to operate its only preserved section recourse would have to be made to ex-Great Eastern engines. But the Preservation Society, in raising funds for the rescue and restoration of a 'J15' 0-6-0 and of the sole remaining ex-G E R 4-6-0, were securing for posterity in Norfolk two historic locomotives, and one at least that was no stranger to M & G N tracks. When the L N E R took over the locomotive department in 1936, the existing power

was considerably extended. For the through workings to Leicester the M & G N had borrowed two Midland class '3' superheated 4-4-0s of the Johnson 'Belpaire' design, and they were much appreciated. In 1936, however, L N E R classes from all three sections of the Southern Area were drafted on to the Joint Line.

I can readily believe reports that the local men did not like the Gresley 'K2' Moguls. Though they would have been by far the most powerful engines that had yet worked on the line, the pony truck did not give much guidance on curves and of those there were plenty. Moreover, they had a harsh and uncomfortable action as well as little in the way of cab comfort, as I experienced from many runs I had on their footplates in Scotland. From the Great Central came some 'D9' Robinson superheater 4-4-0s — a smaller version of the celebrated 'Director' class — but still not considered as good as a Midland class '3'

'Belpaire'; then finally, so far as eight-wheeled engines were concerned there were the rebuilt 'Claud Hamilton' class 4-4-0s, L N E R class 'D16/3'. As small-power express passenger jobs the latter were lovely engines. They were well enough known in Norfolk, for apart from the ordinary work-a-day stud, there were two of them, painted green and kept in immaculate condition at Kings Lynn for working the L N E R Royal Train to and from Sandringham. But with coupled wheels as large as 7 ft 0 in. they were not ideal for the heavy gradients of the Joint Line where there was no opportunity for their speeding proclivities to be used.

Their six-coupled counterparts were another thing altogether. Gresley's modernization of the Holden 4-6-0 produced a beautiful medium-powered express engine, and when one or two of these were made available for working the 'Leicesters', the M & G N men were really delighted. So it is a happy circumstance that the last one of these to remain in service, and which the preservation society has secured, should be one that actually worked over the Joint Line, B R No. 61572. She arrived at Sheringham more than ten years ago, and the first steps towards restoration began; but it has been a long haul for the stalwarts who undertook the job, and before referring in detail to the work done on this engine the actual line itself must be seen in its present context and activity.

The restored G E R 0-6-0 No. 564 passing Sheringham Golf Course with a train for Weybourne, September 1980   *Brian Fisher*

NO
ENTRY

46

It runs for three miles from Sheringham, within sight of the coast, to Weybourne, two-thirds of the mileage of the Bluebell Railway, and in a fascinating and relatively remote part of East Anglia. One would not include Sheringham as one of the more glamorous modern resorts, and most of us, I think, are glad that it is not. It is set in lovely country, and a ride on its railway is every bit as exciting as one through the Kent or Sussex countryside. And while work on the big 4-6-0 goes steadily on—costing, incidentally, more than £10,000—what hauls the trains on the North Norfolk?

The second historic steam locomotive that the Society owns is one of a class that passed almost unnoticed by the railway enthusiast fraternity as a whole when there were many of them doing innumerable humdrum jobs over East Anglia. The 'J15' class of 0-6-0, 'Y14' in the Great Eastern classification, was actually the most numerous of any entering L N E R ownership in January 1923. There were then 272 of them. The design was first introduced by T. W. Worsdell, as early as 1883, but it was so generally successful that construction continued to the same drawings with only minor modifications down to 1913. Engine No. 564, now in service on the North Norfolk Railway, is one of the last built; it dates from 1912, and is one of a batch fitted with both Westinghouse and vacuum brakes. In spite of the class representing more than 20 per cent of the total locomotive stock of the Great Eastern Railway they are not so much as mentioned by E. L. Ahrons in his famous series of articles in the *Railway Magazine* in 1918, when he devoted six instalments of 'Locomotive and Train Working in the Latter Part of the Nineteenth Century' to the Great Eastern. Yet with the 2-4-0 and the 0-6-0 tank classes represented by exhibits in the National Railway Museum, they were about the most generally useful and long-lived engines the Company ever had.

0-6-0 locomotive class J15 No. 564 running round at Weybourne station, the author on the footplate
Brian Fisher

There was certainly nothing in the way of a museum atmosphere in the spring of 1978 when the enthusiasts of the North Norfolk Railway invited me to go to Sheringham, and then to ride out to Weybourne on the footplate of No. 564. It was cold and windy out there, so near to the North Sea, and I thought involuntarily of the comfort and warmth of the diesel cab in which I had ridden from Liverpool Street to Norwich on the previous afternoon. But who with a love of locomotives would not exchange the cosiness of a modern diesel or electric for the rigours of steam, even on so 'sea-breeze-conditioned' a footplate as that of No. 564. With me in the cab came Bill Harvey, long District Locomotive Superintendent at Norwich, under whose vigilance so many steam locomotives have been reconditioned and brought up to first-class working condition. With no more than two coaches we did not have to work very hard on the way out to Weybourne, over tracks where the Cromer portion of the M & G N 'Leicester' used to run; and the return, tender first, was even more air-conditioned!

With mostly volunteer labour, and expert professional guidance, it had taken more than eight years to get No. 564 back from her near-scrap state to working order, but the subsequent history of the engine in traffic proved an object lesson in the problems that have to be faced in rescuing old locomotives from near-death. In her last years in British Railways service she had accumulated a high mileage since general repair. As steam was on the way out, such repairs as she had needed to keep her going had not been done with the care and attention previously given to steam locomotives; and although after arrival at Sheringham in June 1967, the major tasks, such as replacement of the firebox and the building of an entirely new water tank for the tender, had been attended to with the utmost care and skill, and many other points rectified, it was not until the engine was steamed and went back into traffic that other defects were revealed. Some of these, such as steam blows from the pistons and valves, could be tolerated. The leakage was of no consequence from the tractive point of view when the loads to be hauled were so light. The trouble was that it was bad for prestige. No steam locomotive engineer likes to see steam blowing past the glands, and it is of course a defect that gets progressively worse. There were also problems with certain components of the Westinghouse brake system.

The engine had to be taken out of traffic again, after no more than seventy return trips to Weybourne, because a number of the firebox stays were found to be leaking. The boiler cladding sheets had to be removed to gain access to them, and this meant dismantling the whole cab structure, together with many pipes and fittings. When the boiler and the new inner firebox were subjected to a hydraulic pressure test at 240 lb per sq. in., 50 per cent greater than the normal working pressure, both were found to be perfectly safe. The trouble lay in the connecting up of the new inner firebox with the old outer shell; in using modern methods some of the workmanship was not of the best. It was evident that, despite every care, there was likely to be trouble with leaky stays; but unless the engine was to be out of traffic for long periods for these troubles to be rectified it was essential for the cladding sheets to be redesigned so that they could be removed without dismantling half the engine first! So new cladding sheets had to be designed, manufactured and fitted. In passing, it seems evident that leaky stays had not been much of a trouble on the old Great Eastern Railway, or this method of fastening the cladding sheets on these engines would have been changed long ago. The outcome of all this necessary work at Sheringham was that the engine was not returned to traffic until December 1979. And now the volunteer work-force is concentrating its energies upon the 'B12-3' 4-6-0 express engine.

It is natural, of course, that in any railway activity attention becomes concentrated upon the locomotives, for after all it was the performance and success of the *Rocket* at Rainhill in 1829 that was the catalyst in setting the entire railway industry going. Here in North Norfolk, however, I feel that the memory of William Marriott must be kept alive. For after all he *was* the Joint Line for more than forty years, as civil engineer, mechanical engineer, and eventually traffic manager as well. As a pioneer in the use of reinforced concrete he should be especially remembered. As on most railways at the turn of the century, and for some time after, signalling came under Marriott's jurisdiction, as civil engineer, and the centre-balanced arm of Great Northern pattern was the most usual form of semaphore. While there may not be much opportunity to include any of his reinforced concrete specialities in the equipment of the restored stretch of line between Sheringham and Weybourne, he was, I believe, one of the first, if not *the* first in Great Britain to install concrete sleepers on a main line, while there is a celebrated photograph of a stretch of line including no fewer than ten different articles in reinforced concrete. These were: sleepers, stools for point rod rollers, gradient post, post for wire fencing, post for level crossing gates, milepost, stays for gate posts, small crossing number post, point crank stool, and signal post. Several examples of centre-balanced semaphore signal arms and their fittings have been recovered and are at Sheringham. It would be good if a Marriott concrete post could be located, and eventually erected on the restored section of the North Norfolk Railway.

DART VALLEY

Fifty-five years ago, with my parents, I went to spend a fortnight's holiday at Paignton. It was to be a rather special occasion, because it was my last holiday before I went to work at Westinghouse in London. Some weeks previously I had bought several one-inch Ordnance Survey maps, as always I took a push-bike with me and with everything relatively close at hand it was so much easier to jump on the old 'grid' as and when I wished rather than to use public transport. And so, having arrived in Paignton in the afternoon of a beautiful July day, I did not even wait until the next day before setting out for Dartmouth. I saw how the single-tracked branch line twisted and turned as it climbed the cliffs overlooking Torbay; I stopped to notice the junction layout at Churston, where to take the subsidiary branch to Brixham one had to reverse direction, and so, over the hills and down to that breathtaking first sight of the Dart, and then of Kingswear and Dartmouth facing each other across that exquisite estuary, serene in the mellow evening sunshine of high summer. The railway beyond Paignton was then very much of a branch. Although many trains conveyed through carriages to Kingswear the largest engines that were allowed were the '45XX' 2-6-2 tanks, and all the express trains had to change engines at Paignton.

I was not at all concerned with the past history of that line, except that I knew at one time it had been broad gauge, and there were sections of Brunel's bridge rails on longitudinal sleepers in some of the sidings. Had I gone into things a little more deeply I should have found that the South Devon Railway, notorious for the disastrous experiment with atmospheric traction, built a branch line from Newton Abbot no further than Torre, which was then the station for Torquay, and that the line southwards was an enterprise of an initially independent concern, the Dartmouth and Torbay Railway. It was closely enough associated with the South Devon, Brunel was the Engineer, and it was opened through to Kingswear in 1886. Little could one have imagined, seeing the many well-patronized trains that went down there, that a time would come when the nationalized British Railways would seek to close the line beyond Paignton, and that the original name 'Dartmouth and Torbay Railway' would emerge once again, as one of the private railways of Britain.

Torbay did not, however, see the first enterprise in railway preservation in South Devon, because late in 1966 the Dart Valley Light Railway Co. Ltd was formed to restore passenger services on the nine and a half mile branch from Totnes to Ashburton. This line, also broad gauge, had been opened as an independent company, the Buckfastleigh, Totnes and South Devon Railway, in 1872. Ashburton, its terminus, is an ancient town that sent members — yes, in the plural! — to Parliament from the reign of King Edward I; but its trade as an old stannary town, and a centre of the woollen trade in the west, had been rather overtaken, particularly in the latter by Buckfastleigh, and in the nineteenth century there were prospects of good business on a railway connection with the South Devon main line at Totnes. It was significant of where the trade principally lay that Buckfastleigh and not Ashburton was included in the original title of the line. Nevertheless the connecting point with the main line a quarter of a mile east of Totnes was at Ashburton Junction, and in semaphore signalling days on the Great Western it had its own signal box.

Contracts for the purchase of the line were exchanged between British Railways and the Dart Valley Light Railway Co. Ltd towards the end of 1966, and B R applied for a Light Railway Order which in due course was transferred to the operating company. But before that time a considerable amount of rolling stock from the former Great Western Railway had been accumulated and stored on the branch, mostly at Buckfastleigh, and this included many items owned by the Great Western Society, or members of that Society individually, because at that time the running shed at Didcot had not been made available to the Society. The collection included upwards of twenty locomotives, and as many carriages, though some of the larger units, including the 'Castles' *Pendennis* and *Clun,* were not static at Buckfastleigh. At the beginning of 1967 the Dart Valley Railway had seven locomotives of its own, or owned by individual members of the Company, including two 0-4-2 tanks, four 0-6-0 pannier tanks, and one 2-6-2 tank of '45XX' class. It was a good start.

Nevertheless, much work had to be done before the railway could be re-opened in its new form. Under 'light railway' conditions the Dart Valley trains could not enter the main line station at Totnes, and a new platform was built on the branch, just beyond Ashburton Junction, and

named Totnes Riverside. Passenger trains had to be of the push-pull type, for which of course the ex-G W R locomotives already collected at Buckfastleigh were well suited. Because of the cutting short of the line at Totnes, Buckfastleigh was chosen as the headquarters of the new organization. There was some uncertainty about the developing situation at Ashburton, because of an arterial road project — which in the event proved only too well founded. Special trains worked through to Ashburton, but no passenger service was restarted. Some of us had high hopes that the threatened disruption of the line north of Buckfastleigh would be averted, because at Ashburton there was a fine example of a Brunelian all-over roof. Though it might have presented some problems in preservation, it would have made a splendid terminus for the line, as a fine example of railway archaeology.

As it was, the negotiations with British Railways and the Ministry of Transport took far longer than was anticipated, and the granting of a Light Railway Order was repeatedly delayed. The Ministry was also involved in the proposed widening of the A38 road, bringing it up to dual carriageway standard; and part of the railway property north of Buckfastleigh would probably be required to provide the necessary space. Eventually, so as not to delay the opening of the line, the Ministry agreed to the sale of the line between Ashburton Junction (Totnes) to Milepost 7, at the Ashburton end of Buckfastleigh station. So the line was opened for traffic on 5 April 1969; but an ironical twist was given to a special ceremonial occasion six weeks later when Lord Beeching, of all people, unveiled a memorial plaque at Buckfastleigh station, and travelled to Totnes and back in a special train full of invited guests. He had recently retired from his position as Chairman of the British Railways Board and had been raised to the peerage.

His genial personality was fully equal to the occasion, and his felicitous speech showed that he was thoroughly enjoying the whole affair, not least the trip down to Totnes and back. I was one of the guests of the Company on this occasion, and from the rolling stock used and preserved at Buckfastleigh it was evident that it was intended to keep a purely branch line atmosphere on the rejuvenated railway. The train included two of the special luxury saloons previously kept for the ocean specials from Plymouth, on which such exciting running was often made between Millbay Docks and Paddington. The special also included a first class Pullman car, as well as three ordinary third class carriages. At that time the run-round loop at Totnes Riverside had not been laid in, and so the train had a locomotive at each end, as in the early days on the Bluebell Railway. For the record the engines were 2-6-2 tank No. 4555 and 0-6-0 Pannier tank No. 6412.

Two years later the Dart Valley line was a somewhat unlikely inclusion in a tour of West Country interests during the annual summer convention of the Institution of Railway Signal Engineers. After visiting a manufactory of ultra-modern equipment at Plymouth the party was conveyed by road to Buckfastleigh, and thence by special train down the line to Totnes and back. By that time, however, the party was in gala mood, not to be worried by the absence of anything remotely like modern signalling on the railway. The principal diversion, and apprehension on the part of some members, came when I was invited to ride on the footplate and drive the special train. I got them safely back to Buckfastleigh!

The *Flying Scotsman*, visiting the Torbay line, is crossing Greenway Viaduct with a train from Kingswear to Paignton, September 1973   *David Eatwell*

In 1974, in company with many supporters of the old Great Western Railway, I was surprised to learn that a B R standard 2-6-4 tank engine had been acquired from Barry scrap yard, and was going to Buckfastleigh for renovation. It seemed to me from this that the railway was beginning to depart from its true Great Western nature. I would not say a word against the B R 2-6-4 tank as a locomotive — an excellent design in every way — but in bringing one to Buckfastleigh it was introducing an alien influence, and losing the chance of having, in South Devon, a living replica of what a Great Western branch line was like. The trend was continued later when an ex-L N E R buffet car was acquired, and restored to the famous varnished teak livery — superb, but not on the Dart Valley!

On New Year's Day 1973 the Dart Valley Railway Company took over operation of the Paignton-Kingswear line, restoring the original name of the section, Dartmouth and Torbay. The separation of this beautiful stretch of railway from the British Railways main line network is thought-provoking, because in some ways it existed from the time when I first visited the district. In the bursting enterprise of Sir Felix Pole's time as General Manager of the G W R a sustained attempt was made to change all this. The underline structures on the line were strengthened so that even 'King' class engines could work down to Kingswear. It was only a question of taking the weight; there was no question of side clearance! The route had been built for the broad gauge. It was not 'double red' in the civil engineer's route classification, and with this improvement there was no need for the through expresses to change engines at Paignton. The 'King' class engines stationed at Newton Abbot worked the Torbay express right through between Kingswear and Paddington.

Following the ceremony to mark the restoration of ex-G W R 4-6-0 No. 7827 *Lydham Manor*, this engine, assisted by 2-6-2T No. 4555, heads a special train from Kingswear to Paignton, April 1973   *David Eatwell*

An even bigger improvement at Paignton was the construction of a large nest of sidings abreast of Goodrington Sands for carriage stabling. Not all expresses went through to Kingswear, and when I first observed the workings in 1925–6 the empty stock of trains terminating at Paignton had to be worked back empty to Newton Abbot, thus involving extra movements and tiresome occupation of the line with empty stock trains at times of great pressure. But even when the source of inconvenience and delay at Paignton was removed it did not encourage traffic on the single line section. In view of the eventual British Railways decision to close the line it is interesting to read how an entirely non-technical writer, Percy Russell FSA, refers to the railway connection in his beautiful book, *Dartmouth — a History of the Port and Town*. He explains how Charles Seale-Hayne, and his uncle Sir Henry Seale, promoted the Dartmouth and Torbay Railway as an entirely independent enterprise and secured the services of Brunel as Engineer. They wanted the line to cross the Dart near the Greenway Ferry, and so arrive on the Dartmouth side of the estuary; but they were defeated by the obstructionist tactics of certain landowners, and so had to stay on the left bank of the river.

As it was, to quote Percy Russell: 'Any observant traveller will see that the line skirting Torbay, with its changing geological strata, is a very difficult piece of engineering — to say nothing of the tunnel and the rocky ledge cut out to carry the single line to Kingswear. £90,000 was the original estimate of cost, but six years' work was necessary and no less than £262,000 expended.' For no more than ten miles of single line this was a lot of money in the 1860s. Russell, writing in 1949, sums up the economic position of the line succinctly: 'Judging by the published reports of the meetings, the heavy capital cost did not earn much of a return; for in 1870 the line was leased to the South Devon Company for only £10,000 a year: and about ten years later it was absorbed by the Great Western Company. Apart from the difficult gradients and the limitations of the single track, a special obstacle to its heavy use developed through the great expansion of the seaside resorts of Torquay and Paignton. The service of these has long been the prime consideration, and the extension to Kingswear regarded as somewhat of a nuisance.' How true!

Nuisance was certainly the word as far as the locomotive department was concerned. The gradients between Kingswear and Paignton were not so bad as on the South Devon main line, but two miles of 1 in 66–75, including a nasty slippery tunnel could be a killing start to a long run; and although from the engine diagramming point of view it was convenient to send the locomotive for the 'Torbay Express' down from Newton Abbot to Kingswear first thing in the morning prior to its working right through to Paddington, 'Kings' and 'Castles' were not ideal engines for the shocking gradients of the Torbay line. After all they were *express* engines, and it was rather like using a Rolls-Royce where a Land Rover would have been more suitable. I have the most vivid recollections of a day when I had a pass to ride the engine of the 'Torbay' through from Kingswear to Paddington, and I recall as much the laboured pounding at 21 mph up that initial gradient, by the *Earl St Aldwyn*, as the effortless racing at 75 to 85 mph later in the journey. 'Halls', 'Granges' and 'Manors', with their smaller wheels and different valve gear, were much more suitable for the 'Dartmouth and Torbay' line, and they are used there today.

Now that this line is operated by the Dart Valley Light Railway Co. Ltd one could hardly imagine a more ideal location for a steam railway. Percy Russell in his book tends to blame the great popularity of Torquay and Paignton, and the attention given by the Great Western Railway and the Western Region to the traffic thence for the apparent neglect of the rest of the line to Kingswear, rather suggesting that had this been not so the line beyond Paignton might have been developed to something nearer modern standards. But he, of course, was looking at it from the viewpoint of Dartmouth, rather than of the line as a whole. By way of comparison, can one imagine what an advantage it would be to the Bluebell Railway if it had been on the outskirts of Brighton, or to the Kent & East Sussex had it been located in Thanet? Beside Torbay one has, so to speak, a captive clientele on the doorstep. The force of this argument was to be seen when the London Midland Region of British Railways decided to put on the twice-weekly 'Cumbrian Coast Express'. It was felt that only dedicated enthusiasts would drive their cars or travel by connecting trains to Carnforth, the steam metropolis of the North-West, and it was a stroke of genius to start that most attractive of 'specials' from Blackpool, where there was a very large, transient holiday population all through the summer. The train is diesel-hauled to Carnforth where diesel is replaced by steam and it is a 'sell-out' every time it runs.

Those carriage sidings beside Goodrington Sands have proved an invaluable exchange point between the Western Region of British Railways and the Dartmouth and Torbay line, for while the purely local steam trains of the latter start from a separate bay platform in Paignton station, the connections in the sidings to the south are used on occasions when through special excursions from further afield are run to Kingswear. Then the motive power is changed from the B R diesel to the 'Dartmouth and Torbay' steam at Goodrington.

The ex-G W R 2-8-0T No. 5205 crossing Greenway Viaduct on the heavy gradient out of Kingswear, July 1978   *Brian Morrison*

The largest and most powerful steam locomotive at present working on the line is the beautifully restored 4-6-0 No. 7827 *Lydham Manor*, with 'Great Western' and the coat of arms splendidly rendered on the tender, but some of the excursion trains that British Railways bring to the line are too heavy for this engine to take over the severe gradients on its own, and double heading has to be adopted. The assistant engine is then a '45XX' class 2-6-2 tank. The turntable at Kingswear, which was large enough to accommodate a 'King', has now been removed, and *Lydham Manor* has to make one half of its return trip to Kingswear travelling tender first.

Talking of power, I was rather shocked to learn recently that one of the 'Western' class diesel-hydraulic locomotives has found at least a temporary home at Kingswear and may be used on the Dartmouth and Torbay Railway. As many readers will know, I am very far from an 'all-steam' devotee, and over the years it has been my pleasure to record the prowess of the diesel locomotive fleet on British Railways; but while I applaud the efforts of enthusiasts to preserve and maintain in running order an example of a locomotive design that has played a distinguished part in Western Region motive power history I do think that a diesel is an unwarranted intrusion on the Torbay line. It destroys the whole character of the enterprise. Just imagine the feelings of a visitor from afar who made a trip to the 'Torbay Steam Railway', as it is sometimes called, to find that his train was to be hauled by a diesel! I am afraid I should want my money back!

Before the line was divorced from British Railways I recall a very enjoyable Sunday excursion to Kingswear on a train originating at Swindon, when we were hauled by no less a Great Western celebrity than the *City of Truro*. That was in those happy days when that engine was restored, not only to first class working condition, but to the ornate Dean livery. I had the privilege of riding on her footplate through from Bristol to Kingswear. With a substantial train of eight modern coaches, some 280 tons all told, we had to take a pilot over the heavy gradients of the Torbay line. From Newton Abbot, with one of the big 2-6-2 tanks coupled on ahead — not the '45XX' used now, but the far larger and more powerful '41XX' — we, on the veteran, could afford to take things easily on the banks, and leave most of the work to the pilot. Returning in the evening *City of Truro* led the way, and in her gorgeous colouring, in brilliant sunshine, she made a brave show in that lovely Devon countryside.

Locomotives or not, it is one of the most delightful short railway rides one can make, from Paignton to Kingswear, but it is one of those routes on which a sightseer needs to change from the left-hand to the right-hand side of the carriage after Churston, or Brixham Road as that station used to be named when the broad gauge line was first opened. Going south, from the left-hand window, a glorious prospect over the whole of Torbay opens out as the train climbs at 1 in 71 at first, and then at 1 in 60. Gradually the eastward scene begins to include, in the further distance, the red cliffs of East Devon as well as the varied rock formations round the bay itself. Then, having reached the summit of the ridge at Churston station, the descent begins, and on emerging from Greenway Tunnel the widening estuary of the Dart comes into view, far below, luxuriantly flanked with dense woodlands up the steep hillsides on both banks. Speed has always been severely limited from Paignton, and so, with the fair prospect of Dartmouth across the water the train runs slowly along the rocky foreshore to this most delectable terminus — not, one hopes, to find a 'Western' diesel ensconced there!

6

KEIGHLEY AND WORTH VALLEY

The scene now moves further north, but just where is the Worth Valley? Even the celebrated railway author Cecil J. Allen got mixed up once, and wrote of a Midland Scotch Express running at 64 mph up the Worth Valley! The train was actually running over the tracks of the Leeds and Bradford extension line, which the Midland Railway had carried as far as Keighley by 1847, and had continued up Airedale to make an end-on junction with the East Lancashire Railway, at Colne, in 1849. Four year earlier, at the height of the Railway mania, there had been a proposal to build a line over the moors from Hebden Bridge, on the then Manchester and Leeds Railway, to Keighley, but this came to nothing, and it was not until 1861, when a civil engineer, John McLandsborough, visited Haworth and found there was no railway, that more positive steps began. He went to Haworth not in search of possible business but 'as a pilgrim at the shrine of Charlotte Brontë'. With the death of the last member of the family in the same year, the Rev. Patrick, who had been Rector of Haworth for over forty years, the celebrated parsonage had passed into other hands.

John McLandsborough was very much a voice on his own so far as the Brontë sisters were concerned. Throughout the Victorian era female authors were apt to be ostracized. Sir W. S. Gilbert poked fun at them in The Mikado when the Lord High Executioner of Titipu, in compiling his 'little list' of society offenders, included 'that singular anomaly, the lady novelist'; and didn't Mary Ann Evans have to use the pen-name of George Eliot in order to get her work published? It was not until the modern entertainment media of the cinema and television got really into their stride, and portraits of the Brontë sisters appeared on British postage stamps, that the village of Haworth and the wild Wuthering Heights country to the south became a place of pilgrimage. And by then the railway was on the threatened list for closure.

One can be very sure that the hard-headed Yorkshire businessmen whose names appeared on the prospectus of the Keighley and Worth Valley Railway in the autumn of 1861 were not thinking of pilgrim traffic to the Brontë home. There were, even at the outset, fifteen wool mills near the proposed terminus of the line up at Oxenhope; many more were in operation along the route, and it was anticipated that freestone and slate would commence to be quarried once the railway was open. It was intended that the Midland Railway would work the line, in return for 50 per cent of the receipts, and with the business prospects envisaged the K & WV shareholders were expected to receive a dividend of 6 per cent. The Act of Parliament authorizing construction of the line received the Royal Assent in 1862; but although the line was a little less than five miles long it was not until April 1867 that public passenger service began. The estimates for the cost of construction were wildly out, and while a sum of £36,000 was originally allowed for, by the time the line was open no less than £105,000 had been spent. In 1881 the independent company was wound up, and it became part of the Midland Railway.

The misfortunes of the railway between its incorporation in 1862 and its opening, five years later, are recalled more in laughter than in rage and recrimination, thanks to the hilarious account of the work, written in Yorkshire dialect by William Wright, or 'Bill o' th' Hoylus End', as he signed himself. I cannot resist quoting from *Th' History o' Haworth Railway*, his story of how a cow ate the plans, and delayed the construction of the line:

A crookt legg'd pedlar com fra Keighley wun day wi winter-edges, and they tuke him for a sapper and miner et hed cum to mezhur for the railway, and mind yoh they did mak summat on him, they thout that the winter-edges wur the apparatus to mezhur by. But hasumivver, the reyt uns com at after, and a sore disaster they ad yo mind, for they laid the plans o' t'railway dahn at green swarth, and a oud kah belanging to Blue Beard swallowed t'job; they tried to save em but all i vain: a sore do wur this for both folk and the railway, for it put em a year or two back, and folk wur raging mad abaht t'kah, and if it hedn't a been a wizzen'd oud thing they'd a swallowd it alive — the nasty greedy oud thing.

Three years after the Midland had taken over the Keighley and Worth Valley Railway the Great Northern arrived on the scene through a long and continuously curving tunnel that brought it into the valley above Damems, to run parallel to the original line to within half a mile of Keighley. But space was at a premium in and around the junction station, and the Great Northern obtained running powers to make a junction and used Midland metals over that last half-mile. To avoid any chance of congestion the line from the junction was made double-tracked. To what extent, if at all, the

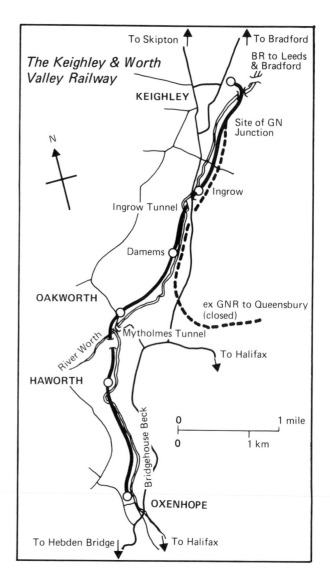

The Keighley & Worth Valley Railway

Great Northern 'invasion' of the Worth Valley was profitable it is not possible to say. Up to the outbreak of World War II, the L N E R was running fifteen trains a day between Keighley and Bradford, taking about forty-five minutes for the fourteen-mile journey. The only station in the valley was at Ingrow, a mile from Keighley itself. Passenger service was withdrawn from this line in May 1955, and apart from the connection at the Keighley end it forms no part of the present story.

I need not go into all the arguments for and against closing the one-time Midland branch line which began in 1959. It is enough to say that despite the most vigorous opposition locally, headed by the Mayor of Keighley, the last passenger train under British Railways management ran on 30 December 1961. Less than three months later, and before the freight service over the line had been withdrawn, the Keighley and Worth Valley Railway Preservation Society was formed, and negotiations were opened to effect the purchase of the line from British Railways. As always in such cases the proceedings were long and complicated; but in due course it was evident to the existing owners that the members of the Preservation Society were not only in deadly earnest, but that they were a fully responsible body. Always when a railway lies out of use for any appreciable time, and no attention is given to work normally covered by routine maintenance, deterioration sets in. But by the beginning of 1964 the Society had shown British Railways enough of their firmness of purpose for permission to be given to members to carry out, entirely on a volunteer basis, various jobs of essential maintenance.

In February 1966 a new company was incorporated, the Keighley and Worth Valley Railway Limited, and early in the following year a formal agreement with British Railways was signed for the purchase of the entire line, except for No. 4 Platform at Keighley station. This was to be leased for twenty-five years. For the record, the purchase price was £45,000. The link-up with British Railways at Keighley was even more advantageous than in the case of the Dartmouth and Torbay at Goodrington sidings, because the new company used the existing station, and through workings to and from the former Midland main line could be very conveniently made. One point of difference from pre-nationalization days was in the re-arrangement of regional boundaries; the line through Keighley was then Eastern instead of London Midland Region. The boundary was at Snaygill, on the main line, just short of Skipton. The necessary Order, declaring the Keighley and Worth Valley to be a Light Railway was obtained by B R, and in 1968 a further order transferring the rights and obligations to the new Company was obtained. The necessary inspection by the Ministry of Transport followed, and only three weeks later, on 29 June 1968, the railway was back in business.

The four years since 1964, when members of the Preservation Society had been permitted to work on the line, had been well spent, and the inaugural train of six carriages was taken up the steep gradients in triumphant style by two immaculate but wildly dissimilar locomotives. The ex-L M S class '2' 2-6-2 tank No. 41241 of the Ivatt era was leading, magnificently turned out in Midland red with the initials K W V R and the Company's new badge on her tank sides, and behind her came the tough American army 0-6-0 shunting tank, in black and yellow brown, with her smokebox and chimney finished in striking aluminium paint.

This inaugural train got away in better style than that of April 1867, by which passenger service on the line was opened for the first time. That train stalled on the first curve out of Keighley station, where the gradient is 1 in 58. Nothing daunted, the Midland driver backed down, right through Keighley station and a little beyond; and then, hey presto, charged back through the station, on to the gradient, and successfully mounted it. But they stuck again, between Oakworth and Haworth, through the engine slipping on wet rails. This time there was no opportunity for going back and taking a run at it. The train was divided and taken to Haworth in two sections. History does not relate the type of engine used on this occasion; but what does excite the imagination is that this dividing operation was carried out some years before the introduction of continuous brakes, and that the rear portion left behind on a 1 in 90 gradient would have needed to be very adequately protected, probably with the wheels scotched, until the engine came back for it. At that date the carriages would probably have been small six-wheelers.

At Haworth engines are being prepared for the day's work: left to right ex-L M S 2-6-2T No. 41241; ex-G W R Pannier tank 0-6-0, and a Hunslet 'Austerity' 0-6-0 *Fred*, July 1973   *David Eatwell*

The first detailed mention of locomotives specifically allocated to the Keighley and Worth Valley line concerns the Midland 0-6-0 tank engines of 1883, of which there were five. They were a typical Johnson design, very handsomely proportioned, and took the place of early 0-6-0 goods tank engines, which had open cabs and a weatherboard on the back of the coal bunker for running in reverse gear. But there were others on which this humane fitting to protect the enginemen's eyes was not in evidence, even though some engines of the class had been reboilered, and had lost their characteristic Johnson mountings in the process. But of course these little class 'I' 0-6-0 tanks were primarily shunting engines, and those that worked on the Worth Valley line were at times interchanged with others on normal yard duties.

On the railways previously described in this book there have been examples of stiff gradients but they have been of a give-and-take nature, particularly on the Dartmouth and Torbay line. There is nothing give-and-take about the Keighley and Worth Valley; it is a continuous gruelling slog from start to finish. The 1 in 66 and 1 in 58 pitch from the start, round the sharp curve from the B R station has already been mentioned. The inclination eases a little over the next mile, to Ingrow Tunnel, but then there is a one and three-quarter mile grind at 1 in 56-64-60 to Oakworth, followed by 1 in 90 and some slightly easier gradients through Haworth station. Then comes the final mile at 1 in 68 up to Oxenhope.

Since the re-opening in 1968 Haworth has been the headquarters of the railway, and the stabling point for the many locomotives and carriages that are now working on the line. The K W V R is certainly a great place to see preserved steam locomotives, either working or resting, because a single-tracked line barely five miles long would not be able to use many of its thirty-two steam locomotives, and its five diesels at the same time.

A remarkably varied collection of steam locomotives has been assembled at Haworth, by no means all ex-L M S types, or their British Railways derivatives, while at times there have been some distinguished visitors. Although now designated a 'light railway' there is nothing 'light' about the track and the underline structures, which permitted use of the very last steam locomotive built for British Railways, the giant '9F' 2-10-0 mixed traffic No. 92220 *Evening Star*. It is, in passing, a testimony to the skill shown in designing such a huge engine as the '9F' that it had such a high route availability; otherwise it would never have been allowed on a line of such continuous and severe curvature as the Keighley and Worth Valley. Other large permanent residents at Haworth are the Stanier '8F' 2-8-0 — a very useful engine with heavy trains on such gradients — and the War Department 'Austerity' 2-8-0. The engine now on the Worth Valley is one that went abroad during the later stages of the

war, and was kept in strategic reserve in Sweden, having been purchased from the Netherlands State Railways in 1951. It was bought back by a group of English enthusiasts in 1973. This locomotive is of particular interest to those whose studies lie beyond Great Britain, because during its stay in Scandinavia it was fitted with an arctic weather-proof cab and snow deflectors in front of the leading wheels.

Many television viewers of the black and white era will remember the charming serial *The Railway Children,* shown about twenty years ago. When EMI decided to make a new version of this, in colour, there were no regular steam trains on British Railways, and certainly no vintage locomotives, so the film-makers came to the Keighley and Worth Valley, for the beautiful scenery as well as the engines. In the film the railway concerned was the fictitious 'Great Northern and Southern' and a special engine livery had to be invented. The locomotive chosen to star in the film was the privately owned Lancashire and Yorkshire Railway veteran of 1887, the Aspinall 0-6-0 goods No. 957, and instead of the black livery she had carried throughout her *seventy-two years* of ordinary railway service she was given a most attractive finish in leaf green, with her coupling rods painted red, and the initials 'G N & S R' on the tender. She looked a real picture. In 1975 at the age of eighty-eight (!) she was repainted to her final British Railways style; and now, if not exactly going 'strong', she is still on the active list of the Keighley and Worth Valley Railway.

The other K & W V locomotive to feature in *The Railway Children* was a comparative youngster. It was one of several 0-6-0 pannier tanks purchased by London Transport from the Western Region — the well-known and numerous Great Western standard design. There were nearly 800 of them — ideal engines for a steeply graded line like the Worth Valley. I shall always remember an enthusiastic driver on one of the Welsh valley lines saying of them: 'They're dynamic!' The engine featured in the film was one of the very first batch, built in 1929. Before going into ordinary passenger service

61

The ex-G N R 'Atlantic' No. 990 *Henry Oakley* as leading engine on a Keighley—Oxenhope train near Haworth. The train engine is another Hunslet 'Austerity' 0-6-0T, from the Longmoor Military Railway, September 1977   *David Eatwell*

Opposite: Train for Keighley leaving Oxenhope hauled by ex-G W R pannier 0-6-0T when painted in London Transport colours, May 1980   *Brian Morrison*

she was painted a golden yellow, very similar to Marriott's 'golden gorse' on the Midland and Great Northern Joint, in North Norfolk. She ran in this attractive style for five years, but when she needed a repaint, the Metropolitan Railway style, euphemistically termed 'bullock-maroon', was used. It is actually a rich red-brown and looks equally attractive. It was familiar to commuters in Metro-land when the residential trains proceeding into the country north of Rickmansworth were still steam-hauled.

The Keighley and Worth Valley certainly has a great variety of locomotive liveries. Unlike some of the other private railways there is no standard style to which all acquisitions are made to conform. In earlier chapters I have referred to the Hunslet

0-6-0 'Austerity' tank engines built in such numbers for the War Department during World War II. The Keighley and Worth Valley acquired five of these excellent general utility tank engines, and they have been a little unkindly nicknamed the 'Uglies'. They are certainly not in the top flight for beauty of outline, but some attempt has been made to compensate for their rather stark functional appearance by decking them in gay, dissimilar colours. One is in Caledonian blue, a second is in pillar-box red, while a third, which came from the Longmoor Military Railway, is black and for some time carried the initials L M R on her saddle tanks. The fourth is a remarkable machine from a colliery near Walkden, Manchester. It is fitted with a 'Klypor' blastpipe and chimney, and a gas-producer firebox, the inventions of an Argentinian engineer, L. D. Porta. The fifth is another of the standard type and is painted dark green.

The ride up the valley from Keighley is a delightful one, especially if, as I was privileged to do, one rides on the footplate of the engine. With a well-patronized excursion train from Lincolnshire two engines were needed, and we had an ex-L M S Ivatt 2-6-2 tank leading and the US Army 0-6-0 shunter next to the train. This latter engine is now oil-fired. At Damems, about three-quarters of a mile beyond Ingrow Tunnel, there is some interesting equipment at the passing loop. This is a traffic working facility that has been added by the new owners. At times business was so brisk that it was desirable to have a passing loop on what would otherwise have been a single line section extending over the three and three-quarter miles from Keighley up to Haworth; and because of the relative slow speeds, both uphill and down, it could take a considerable time. The Damems loop was constructed in 1971, almost entirely with volunteer labour. The signal box, of vintage Midland Railway design, was brought from Frizinghall, Bradford, quite a feat of transportation in itself, and the signals controlling train movements at the loop are also of the standard Midland lower quadrant semaphore type, of which a characteristic feature was to have round discs instead of stripes — white on the red face of the blade, and black on the white back.

Today, with all the bustle and activity of a railway headquarters, with extensive locomotive and carriage sheds, and souvenir shops, cafeteria, and so on for the many visitors, it has not been possible to recreate at Haworth the atmosphere of a nineteenth-century Midland country station, though the original buidings are all there — albeit put to different uses. The steady increase in traffic since the re-opening of the line has brought problems of its own. Never in its earlier working life were passenger trains of such length hauled up to Haworth and Oxenhope, and the track facilities had to be modified accordingly. Furthermore, as the railway is within easy reach of many great centres of population in the West Riding, many visitors come in their cars, and some levelling of the ground in the station approaches at both Haworth and Oxenhope has been made to provide adequate space. One mentions this with bated breath, but more people appear to come to Haworth to see the trains than to make a pilgrimage to the Brontë country!

The Keighley and Worth Valley Railway has always been a willing host to distinguished steam locomotives from other areas, and the B R '9F' 2-10-0 *Evening Star,* normally based at the National Railway Museum, York, has already been mentioned. In 1969 the railway welcomed one of the very first of the famous Stanier 'Black Five' 4-6-0s of the L M S, No. 5025. This engine was only the sixth of the class put into traffic, being of the 5020—5039 batch built by the Vulcan Foundry in 1934. The restored engine, privately owned, had

---

An ex-L M S 'Black Five' 4-6-0 No. 45212 climbing the heavy gradient over Mytholmes Viaduct, June 1976
Brian Morrison

been overhauled by the Hunslet Engine Company prior to going to Scotland. We shall meet her again in Chapter 11 of this book.

But the most distinguished visitor of all was the very first locomotive of the 'Atlantic' class ever to run the rails in Great Britain, the Great Northern No. 990, designed by H. A. Ivatt, father of the designer of the L M S 2-6-2 tanks, and built at Doncaster Plant Works in 1898. This beautiful engine was scheduled for preservation by the L N E R, and after World War II went to the original Railway Museum at York. She was brought out and restored to full working order in 1952 to take part in the celebrations of the centenary of Doncaster works in that year; indeed she made several trips at full express speed between Leeds and Kings Cross. After taking part

in the sesqui-centenary celebrations of the Stockton and Darlington Railway in 1975, she came to the Worth Valley on temporary loan. As she was a Great Northern engine one felt she might have wanted to take the left-hand route at the site of 'GN Junction' outside Keighley, and to climb the bank to Queensbury and so to Bradford, instead of continuing up the Worth Valley to Haworth! But the one-time Great Northern line has long been dismantled. Joking apart, No. 990 *Henry Oakley* made a glorious sight on the Worth Valley line.

At Haworth, the very first British 'Atlantic', ex-G N R No. 990 *Henry Oakley*, on loan from the National Railway Museum, September 1977   *David Eatwell*

7
STEAM CENTRES AND TOURS

Until now I have been writing about private railways, which, by the hard necessity of finance and the limited availability of devoted volunteer staffs, are restricted to quite small operational track mileages. I must now turn, for one chapter, to an activity that is making the enjoyment of steam locomotives available to a far wider circle of enthusiasts, and to well-wishers generally. In January 1976 the *Railway Magazine* reminded its readers that there had been a period up to 1971 when steam specials were banned entirely from any part of British Railways. The article was headed 'Mr Shirley Bows Out'. It began: 'British Railway enthusiasts whose memories go back to the Beeching era will, with their Australian counterparts, shed no tears over the impending retirement of Mr Philip Shirley from the post of Chief Commissioner of the Public Transport Commission of New South Wales . . . Justly or not, he became identified with the negative aspects of Beeching's policies: line closures and withdrawal of services. He was also alleged to be the chief architect of the B R "steam ban" which operated rigidly until October 1971.' He did the same in New South Wales and incurred the wrath of all Australian railway enthusiasts.

The change in attitude on British Railways since Mr Shirley left has been profound. All over the country there were pockets of steam: locomotives preserved, but with no chance of running. Once the ban was removed over a few clearly designated routes, the societies that had been formed to preserve locomotives of their particular affection began to make plans to run them. Inevitably there was some overlapping at first, but it was soon realized by the private owners that there would be everything to be gained by the formation of a single, co-ordinated organization, through which they could negotiate with British Railways as a body, rather than individually. The British Railways Board, for its part, was glad enough to have only one organization to deal with, and since 1975, when the Steam Locomotive Operators Association was formed, the numerous steam trips have been arranged on a yearly basis for all members of the association. While the locomotives assigned to privately organized tour trains are naturally required to be in a condition fit for main line work they are all, without exception, privately owned. British Railways have no steam locomotives of their own, nor any facilities for maintaining them. The locomotives used for such trips are kept in yard areas that have been either leased or purchased from the British Railways Board. Obviously some degree of concentration of facilities was desirable, and several Steam Centres have been established.

The operation of steam locomotives is a highly

complex business; how complex was perhaps not fully realized by many dedicated enthusiasts of the steam era, because the train services were worked with such regularity and reasonably good punctuality. It is often argued by those who have strong partisan views on the steam versus diesel (or electric) controversy that a steam locomotive might have many things wrong with it, but it would still go; whereas a relatively slight failure on a diesel or an electric could put it completely out of action. It is this factor, and the resulting interruption of service, that sometimes leads to the comment that modern power 'is always going wrong', whereas steam was reliable! Some memories are apt to be short. For my own part I can recall many occasions, even in the halcyon days of the later 1930s, when locomotives of the most honoured express passenger classes lost time through minor ailments; but the delays were not enough to cause more than brief passing mention from a few passengers; and there were no loud speakers at principal stations to broadcast an apologia for late running or cancellation. Only those who worked in a big running shed concerned with heavy and fast express workings knew of the extremely complex organization that kept those engines on the road.

The Steam Locomotive Operators Association of today faces many additional problems. None of the engines concerned is new, and the fact that their use is intermittent is a disadvantage rather than a help. Although they are always turned out in spanking condition, so far as external appearance is concerned, defects tend to show up more frequently than on a locomotive newly out-shopped in a regular routine cycle of maintenance, even though a steam locomotive in regular service would be running an immeasurably greater monthly mileage. Furthermore, on the private

On the Furness line of British Railways, a charter-special, Carnforth to Sellafield, crossing the Leven Viaduct near Ulverston, hauled by *Hardwicke* and *Flying Scotsman*, May 1976   *David Eatwell*

In January 1981 the one ex-L M S 'Black Five' 4-6-0 with Stephenson's link motion, No. 4767, on the eastbound Cumbrian Mountain Express, near Clapham, North Yorkshire   *David Eatwell*

lines locomotives are operating under 'light railway' conditions, at an absolute maximum speed of 25 mph. It is of course true that before turning a wheel on a 'light railway' the engines are subject to the same stringent examination of all the parts subject to steam pressure as in their former regular service on British Railways; for while one can struggle home with a big end that is inclined to heat, or an axle-box that is a bit touchy, there must be nothing wrong with the boiler, except perhaps internal leaking of the tube joints or stays. Every railway, however 'light', must have its qualified staff, even though volunteer, who can deal with the day-to-day problems of boiler maintenance; and although there may be many locomotives attached to such organizations some of them are often not in a condition to work passenger trains.

On Saturday 3 August 1968 the last trains in the public time-table to be hauled by steam locomotives ran, in the late evening, from Preston to Blackpool and to Liverpool. Just over a week later, on Sunday 11 August, what Philip Shirley no doubt fondly imagined was the very last steam train to run over British Railways metals was an excursion from Liverpool to Carlisle and back. The curtain then went down with a vengeance; but a week earlier a preserved steam locomotive 'escaped' from a somewhat forlorn retirement to take up a role prophetic of future happenings. This was the extraction, from virtual oblivion at Swindon, of the ever-famous 4-6-0 No. 6000 *King George V*, on the first stage of a journey to Hereford. Under cover of night, and at a speed never exceeding 20 mph this precious load was towed by a diesel to Alexandra Dock Junction, there to go into the works of A. R. Adams & Son for renovation. Renovation for what? H. P. Bulmer Ltd, the famous cider makers, have three-quarters of a mile of private track at Hereford, and there it was planned to steam No. 6000 occasionally, and haul the special 'cider train', consisting of five former B R Pullman cars. The train would go on tour at times, but hauled by non-steam B R power. The 'star' of the whole show, because of the Shirley ban, was not allowed beyond the private track.

Although the Bulmer circuit at Hereford was by no means the first of the Steam Centres — enclaves where preserved locomotives could still be steamed within their precincts — it came to have a very special significance. Even the dark years from 1968 had their moments of delight, and I shall never forget a day in the early spring of 1969 when my wife and I were invited to a little party in the Bulmer cider train. The world-famous artist Terence Cuneo was also one of their guests. His role that day was plain enough: to paint a picture of the *King George V* in action; but when we got to Hereford I learned that I also had a special job: to drive the engine round the circuit, back and forth, to position it for Cuneo. I think we all regretted that the splendid engine could no longer go beyond the precincts. Little did we all imagine that in rather more than two years' time our wildest hopes would be fulfilled. May I quote from some of the concluding paragraphs of my book *Engine 6000* (David & Charles, Newton Abbot):

I was in Canada and the USA for six weeks in the late summer of 1971, but my plane from Pittsburgh had barely touched down at Heathrow before I was receiving telephone messages with the astonishing news that British Railways had made a concession, and the King George V *was to run main line rails again, on the very next day. Unfortunately a*

long absence from home made it impossible for me to dash off to see her on the first leg of that remarkable 'Royal Journey', as the Railway Magazine *called it; but there was still the following weekend. How Bulmer's, and in particular Mr Peter Prior, persuaded British Railways to lift their ban on steam I do not know; but lifted it was, 'to assess the practical difficulties in operating steam-hauled trains over British Railways', as the official announcement read. It was no half-day holiday 'doddle' either. True, the engine was not required to steam up to 25,000 lb per hour once again, or anything like it; but the itinerary, extending over four days, involved the following:*

Oct 2: Hereford to Birmingham (Tyseley) via Severn Tunnel and Oxford

Oct 4: Birmingham (Moor St) to Kensington (Olympia) by the historic route of the one-time two-hour expresses

Oct 7: Olympia to Swindon

Oct 9: Swindon to Hereford, via Bath, Bristol (Stapleton Rd) and Severn Tunnel Junction

To say that this tour was a 'Royal Progress' would be a wild under-statement. I do not think it is far off the mark to say that nothing like it has previously been seen on the railways of this country — or of any other country for that matter. The crowds that thronged the lineside at every point of vantage, and many other points that are not normally accessible, were phenomenal. At times, indeed, they were in danger of getting out of control, to their own peril from other trains.

I was in Hereford on 7 October to give a talk to The 6000 Locomotive Association, and then details were fixed for my own journey with the engine, two days later. I drove my car from Bath to Severn Tunnel Junction to join the train there, and long before coming to the station I met the first manifestations of the extraordinary popularity of the trip as a public spectacle. All road approaches to the station were packed; I could not park my car nearer than half a mile away, and as I subsequently made my way, on foot, I began counting the cars. Having got to 300 I gave up. There must have been

at least double that number in the immediate neighbourhood of the station. Once again I was privileged to ride on the footplate, from Severn Tunnel Junction up to Pontypool Road, and again the words that occurred to me were 'Royal Progress'! From the footplate the lineside was an amazing sight. Young and old, men and women alike in almost equal numbers waved us on our way. This was all the more remarkable because this was not one of the principal express routes of the G W R, and was only worked over by the Kings in their declining years.

It had been enjoyable enough to mount the footplate of No. 6000, as a 'live' engine, in 1969, and to drive her round Bulmer's track; but this was the 'real' thing. In my recent visit to Canada I had ridden many hundreds of miles on the footplate, but on diesels — a 'white collar' job; but on 6000 I was in overalls again, amid all the once-familiar smells of hot oil, the tang of coal dust, and the 'sing' of the injector. She was in superb mechanical condition, running as sweetly as the proverbial sewing machine, though no great output of power was demanded. In addition to the five Pullman cars of this Bulmer exhibition train there were four coaches for ordinary passengers in the rear, 335 tons tare and 350 tons full. Although the point-to-point times were easy, it was important not to get ahead. The passing times at principal intermediate points had been published shortly before the trips, and everyone on board was anxious that no one should miss his or her sight of the train through its running early. Actually one would imagine most of the sightseers had taken up their chosen places some time before the train was advertised to pass.

It was an extraordinary demonstration of popular appeal. The assessment British Railways made of 'the practical difficulties in

On the one-time Furness and Midland joint line, east of Carnforth, a return excursion from Sellafield to St Pancras is passing the dismantled station of Borwick, hauled by 'Black Five' 4-6-0 No. 44932—one of the Carnforth stalwarts, August 1974   *Derek Cross*

operating steam-hauled trains' must have been very favourable, because in 1972 the ban was lifted, and five somewhat lightly used routes were authorized for steam specials. The five routes were:

Birmingham (Moor St) to Didcot
Newport (Mon) to Shrewsbury
York to Scarborough
Newcastle to Carlisle
Carnforth to Barrow

These were chosen because there were turning facilities in the form of triangles at each end, and there were privately owned locomotives belonging to preservation societies, or individuals, nearby. Turntables were being scrapped. In addition to Hereford there were growing Steam Centres at Birmingham (Tyseley shed), Didcot, Dinting and Carnforth. Later in 1972 details were issued of twenty-three locomotives that had been approved by British Railways for running on the selected routes. In addition to the *King George V* there were 9 other Great Western locomotives, including *Pendennis Castle* and *Clun Castle;* 7 ex-L M S 4-6-0s; 3 ex-L N E R 'Pacifics' though not at that time including *Flying Scotsman,* which was in the USA: the Southern 4-6-2 *Clan Line,* and two B R standards, the 2-10-0 *Black Prince* and the class '4' 4-6-0 *Green Knight*. The preserved locomotives were accepted on B R metals subject to the owners indemnifying B R against any mishap, and by the taking out of insurance for an appropriate amount. For all trips B R would provide the driver, fireman and motive power inspectors, and no representatives of the owner would be allowed on the footplate, except by special arrangement. That the special trips proved a great success goes almost without saying, but here I am concerned more with how the Steam Centres themselves were developed to meet the growing requirement for locomotives. For they were, after all, private railways of a very special kind.

The Cumbrian Mountain Express southbound from Carlisle near Armathwaite, hauled ex-L M S 4-6-0 No. 5690 *Leander*, April 1980   *John Titlow*

Stepping for a few paragraphs ahead of that momentous summer of 1972 it is pleasing to note how so many individual preservation enterprises, both of locomotives and stretches of line, have become integrated to a remarkable degree into a unified national activity. For this the formation in 1975 of the Steam Locomotive Operators

Association was responsible. Its object is to promote the continued operation of steam locomotives on British Railways routes by ensuring the maximum co-operation between the locomotive owners, operators and the British Railways Board. Apart from the Steam Centres, all of which are represented in one way or another in the membership of the Association, there are a number of groups supporting the preservation and maintenance of important individual locomotives, whose membership of the Association is invaluable so far as the provision of motive power for special trains is concerned. These include, among others, the 'A4' Locomotive Society, the

Merchant Navy Locomotive Society, and the Princess Elizabeth Locomotive Society — all now formed into limited companies.

One of the most pleasing features of the degree of co-operation that has been engendered by the Association is the way in which preserved locomotives move about nowadays from one Centre to another, and enable different locomotives to be exhibited, or steamed, regardless of their actual ownership. At the time I was drafting this particular chapter I paid one of my periodic visits to the National Railway Museum at York, and found that they had, as one of the majestic group posed round Turntable A, a North Eastern Railway class 'P3' 0-6-0 mineral engine, owned by the North Eastern Railway preservation group. I enquired after several notable members of the national collection which were not in evidence and was informed where they had been loaned, for use on special trains in some cases.

In the very dawn of the industry, a swarm of individual railways grew up all over the country, quite unconnected and unrelated to each other; and as they extended and linked up their activities they became co-ordinated and their financial returns were sorted out by the Railway Clearing House. So today, the efforts in locomotive preservation and running were once unco-ordinated but the Steam Locomotive Operators Association is now acting as the clearing house, as between the various individual interests.

I cannot pass beyond my references to SLOA without mention of two men who have been largely responsible for bringing the running of privately owned steam locomotives on British Railways to a high degree of efficiency, and in cordial relations with the British Railways Board. First of all there is George Hinchcliffe, the Chairman of the Association, who, as engineer in charge of the tour of *Flying Scotsman* in the USA, gathered as much experience as any man living of the trials and tribulations of running a preserved locomotive, and of the inevitable politico-public relations involved. Secretary of the Association is Bernard J. Staite, first involved in the great activity when the *King George V* went to Hereford in 1971; and as a result of his early experience with that engine, and his association with the Swindon men, mostly in retirement, who gave their services so readily, he has done much to establish the professional status of the Association.

The privately owned Steam Centres and their locomotives were, from 1972 onwards, the source of an ever-increasing and very popular series of excursions over British Railways' routes; and while there were undoubtedly some who 'did not want to know' about steam, there were also acute observers who realized that in the running of steam specials there was good business to be had. So, in 1978, ten years after British Railways had run their 'last steam train', the London Midland Region announced the forthcoming running of the 'Cumbrian Coast Express', steam-hauled between Carnforth and Sellafield. I must not at this stage steal the thunder of my later chapter, which is reserved for the most spectacular of the Steam Centres, Carnforth, and for the men and women who work there, except to say that such was the confidence B R had in the management of that Centre that they were ready enough to hire the privately owned locomotives based there.

At the time of writing it is expected that the sphere of activity of steam specials organized by British Railways will be greatly extended, to involve trips on the Western and Scottish Regions and making use of many more privately owned steam locomotives, working from a large number of privately managed Steam Centres. The formula is infectious!

8

NORTH YORKSHIRE MOORS

It is one of the strange features of the geography of England that with the exception of the River Esk at Whitby there is no port or river mouth of the slightest consequence anywhere in the hundred miles of the east coast from the Tees to the Humber. Such rivers as rise within a few miles of the sea inland from Scarborough and Filey flow westward to join the Derwent. The reason is to be found in the almost continuous range of high ground that flanks the North Sea. Even in the case of Whitby, although the Esk is a considerable stream nearing its mouth, it is short and has its head waters in the high moorlands little more than ten miles from the sea. The town of Whitby suffered much from vicissitudes in its staple trade of fishing. It was true that there was a demand for the ironstone mined at Grosmont in the early 1800s, and for timber, but great difficulty was experienced in getting it down to Whitby for shipment. The leading citizens saw that railways were proving advantageous to ports like Stockton and Liverpool, and they approached George Stephenson to advise upon a possible railway up the Esk Valley, and then over the high moors to Pickering.

It was an extraordinary project — so unlike anything with which George Stephenson had been associated. Money was tight. The capital was raised entirely locally, and no more than a single line of rails could be afforded. The Whitby and Pickering Railway Company secured their Act of Incorporation without any difficulty in May 1833. No one else seemed interested in that remote locality. Furthermore, locomotive haulage was to be prohibited and horses were used instead. To get up on to the moors from Grosmont to Goathland on a gradient of 1 in 15, cable haulage was used; and although it took about two and a half hours to do the twenty-five miles from Whitby to Pickering in 1836 when the line was opened, most people seemed to be satisfied. It was vastly better than struggling over the atrocious moorland tracks. But the shareholders were not satisfied, and they were glad enough in 1845 when George Hudson came along and quickly concluded negotiations for the line's absorption by the York and North Midland Railway. Whitby was now linked into the rest of the Hudson 'empire'. Two years later locomotive haulage took the place of horses, though the notorious 1 in 15 incline from Grosmont up to Goathland was worked by cable, until there was a serious accident in February 1864. A cable broke, and a passenger train ran at high speed down to derailment, causing the death of several people. By that time, however, the railway had become part of the North Eastern, and a deviation line, with a maximum gradient of 1 in 49, was built soon afterwards. This could be

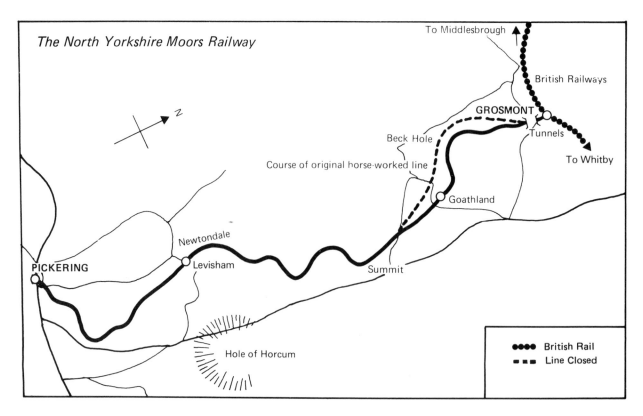

The North Yorkshire Moors Railway

To Middlesbrough

British Railways

GROSMONT

Beck Hole

Course of original horse-worked line

Tunnels

To Whitby

Goathland

Newtondale

Levisham

Summit

PICKERING

Hole of Horcum

●●●● British Rail
■ ■ ■ Line Closed

worked by locomotives in the course of a journey through from Whitby to Pickering and beyond.

Whitby did not escape the closures of the Beeching era. The coastal route from Scarborough to Saltburn, crossing the Esk Valley at Whitby on a fine thirteen-arch red-brick viaduct, was one of the victims, and it was evidently considered that Whitby itself did not need more than one rail outlet. At Grosmont the original line to Pickering and the south was joined by the inland route from Middlesbrough, coming down the Esk Valley, and this was the route chosen to be kept in operation by B R. But the impending closure of so historic a line as that over the moors to Pickering led to the formation, in 1967, of a preservation society, and this led eventually to the establishment of the North Yorkshire Moors Railway, with a strong flavour of the old North Eastern Railway. One look at the gradient profile of the line is enough to suggest that it would be no light task for preserved

steam locomotives to haul modern passenger trains over such a route, and even when the coaches were no larger than four-wheelers and there weren't many of them, the physical nature of the line in its frequent and severe curvature superimposed upon the heavy gradients led to the introduction of some highly individual designs of locomotive.

The North Eastern Railway was foremost among the old companies of Great Britain in the preservation of ancient rolling stock, partly because it had Boards of Directors and General Managers who were proud of their heritage dating back to the Stockton and Darlington, and which, as a major constituent of the L N E R had a notable part to play in the Railway Centenary of 1925. Three historic locomotives, a Fletcher 7 ft 2-4-0 express, a Stockton and Darlington long-boilered 0-6-0 goods and a Tennant 2-4-0, were restored to original condition, and later formed a splendid nucleus of the exhibits in the old Railway Museum at York. It was not likely, however, that one of the most distinctive of all locomotives to run on the Whitby and Pickering line, namely the very quaint 'Whitby bogie' 4-4-0s of 1864—5, could have been resuscitated. Fletcher designed them in readiness for through running between Whitby and Pickering when the deviation line, with its 1 in 49 gradient, was opened. They had very small coupled wheels of only 5 ft 2 in. diameter; and although Fletcher did not otherwise design any bogie engines he was sufficiently impressed with the extraordinarily curvaceous nature of this line to break his rule. But instead of putting the bogie centre beneath the smokebox as was usual on most contemporary and subsequent designs of 4-4-0, he set it back, so that the leading wheels came under the smokebox, and gave a correspondingly shorter rigid wheelbase. Some of these sturdy little engines put in nearly thirty years of hard work on the Whitby and Pickering line.

When my friends of the Tees-side Branch of the Stephenson Locomotive Society took me, two years ago, to Grosmont to join a special train on the North Yorkshire Moors Railway, and I saw the remarkable variety of locomotives assembled there, I was reminded of the photographic activities of Dr T. F. Budden towards the end of the nineteenth century, and how, unlike many of his contemporaries, he sought out the remoter sheds in search of quaint survivals. At Whitby he had a rich haul. Outside the shed there were six locomotives, all looking as though they had been polished ready to haul the Royal Train, but all of six widely differing designs. He was evidently too late to catch one of Fletcher's 'Whitby bogie' 4-4-0s, the last of which had been scrapped in 1893, but he certainly 'copped' a 0-6-0 saddle tank, built in 1866, and still in its original condition. The ex-

A group at Grosmont on 5 May 1979, prior to special run to Pickering to celebrate the 80th birthday of the G N R saddle tank 0-6-0 No. 1247, and the 70th anniversary of the founding of the Stephenson Locomotive Society. In centre of group, R. I. Armstrong, Tees-side S L S Chairman; the author; and Captain W. G. Smith, the owner of the locomotive
S L S Tees-side Centre Collection

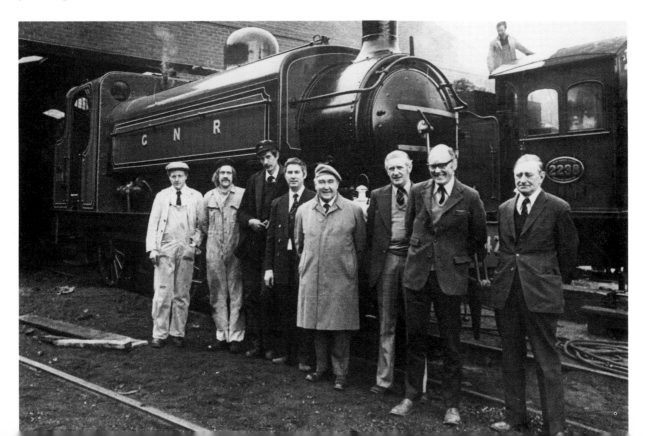

Stockton and Darlington long-boilered 0-6-0 goods were no rarities at Whitby, indeed I found one there in 1922 and photographed it — the very one that was subsequently restored to its original condition for the 1925 Centenary. Tank engines of the 0-4-4 and 2-4-2 types were in regular use on passenger trains at the turn of the century, but when G. W. J. Potter wrote of the Whitby and Pickering Railway in the *Railway Magazine* in 1900, he referred to the McDonnell 4-4-0s, some of which had been drafted on to the line to replace the old 'Whitby bogies'.

When the McDonnell 4-4-0s were first introduced in 1884, prejudice among the enginemen set them down as among the world's worst; and their stay on the main line express workings was brief. But though not powerful enough for the heaviest work they were excellent engines in themselves, and by their wheel arrangement well suited to a line with many curves. A few of them were sent to Whitby. Of them Potter wrote: 'These engines are very neat looking and well able to take the heavy trains up the steep inclines.' But Potter was something of a historian as well as a railway enthusiast and, noting one of the McDonnell 4-4-0s was numbered 664 — duly photographed, I may add, by Dr Budden — he recalled that it commemorated the date of the Council held at Whitby Abbey in AD 664 to settle the dispute between the Irish and the Roman Churches as to the proper time for keeping Easter. One hardly imagines that this was in mind when engine No. 664 was allocated to Whitby shed!

I first travelled over the Whitby and Pickering line in 1922. Apart from summer excursions the service was quite local, and right down to the outbreak of World War II there was only one train a day that brought a through carriage from Leeds. In 1922 this was usually worked by an 'F' class 4-4-0, a slightly smaller edition of that beautiful 'M' class No. 1621 that adorns the National Railway Museum at York. Occasionally one saw one of the larger 'R' class, but otherwise the passenger service over the very severe road from Grosmont over Goathland Moor was worked by

the 'O' class 0-4-4 tank engines. Even in 1900, when Potter wrote his article in the *Railway Magazine*, they were described as: 'The latest type of engine used on the Whitby and Pickering Railway.' When Budden visited Whitby he found only the older type of 0-4-4 tank, the Fletcher 'BTP', which initials stood for 'Bogie Tank Passenger'. Travelling to Whitby on a Saturday afternoon in 1922 by that very heavy and crowded through train from Leeds we were hauled by an 'F' class 4-4-0 which from Pickering took an 'O' class 0-4-4 tank as pilot to climb the heavy gradients over the moors.

These early memories of my own, and evidence of a great variety of locomotives in use in earlier days, form an appropriate introduction to a description of the line since its preservation and re-establishment as a 'light railway'. The first section to be opened was from Grosmont up the 1 in 49 incline to Goathland, running through the North Yorks National Park. The enterprise received very welcome support from local people as well as from railway enthusiasts, and by 1971 the line was open to Pickering. At the outset the Preservation Society was fortunate in obtaining the loan of two notable North Eastern Railway locomotives, acquired by the North Eastern Locomotive Preservation Group and, after withdrawal from British Railways service, housed at Tyne Dock shed. The support which the railway itself received from the first launching of the preservation scheme was an indication that some substantial passenger train loads would have to be hauled up that incline, and the two locomotives that were to be made available were both ideal for the job.

Although the North Eastern Railway took an important and at times spectacular part in the working of the East Coast Anglo-Scottish express passenger service, it was basically a great mineral hauler, and the two locomotives awaiting restoration at Tyne Dock were typical examples of outstandingly successful classes. The first to arrive at Grosmont was the massive 'T2' outside-cylindered 0-8-0 (L N E R class Q6). When first restored and repainted she carried her later

L N E R number, 3395, acquired during the Thompson renumbering of the entire locomotive stock, but she was originally N E R No. 2238, built at Darlington Works in 1918. These locomotives were designed for mighty weight-pulling on steep gradients, and provided a rare example of an engine that could be driven absolutely all-out — full regulator and full fore gear — for indefinite periods at anything up to maximum mineral train speeds. Such performance was not likely to be required, even on the Goathland ascent, but an engine of such capacity was a very useful tool.

The second engine to come from Tyne Dock was one of Wilson Worsdell's 'P3' class 0-6-0s. This is another design of which I have seen some impressive work from the vantage point of the footplate. In addition to the very heavily graded mineral lines, like those up to Consett, the North Eastern Railway had many routes of relatively short hauls from the collieries to the numerous shipping ports on the Northumberland and Durham coast. Thereon was plenty of sharp grading, but none perhaps severe enough to rule the load, and a powerful 0-6-0 was ideal. The 'P3' dates from 1906, and it is significant of their general usefulness that engines of this class

continued to be built until 1923. The engine that is preserved, and restored so splendidly to the North Eastern style of painting for freight engines, No. 2392, is actually the very last to be built, one of a batch of ten turned from Darlington Works in 1923. I have particular memories of these engines, because I rode one of them, old 2384, on a characteristic duty from Blyth North shed. We went out tender first, in the teeth of an icy wind, to collect a heavy load of coal from Ellington Colliery — 700 tons of it — and bring to the staithes at Blyth for dumping into the coastwise colliers. The North Yorkshire Moors Railway made a gala occasion of it when No. 2392 arrived at Grosmont in October 1971, after almost three years had been spent in her restoration. At the moment of writing she is a distinguished visitor to the National Railway Museum at York, standing in her gleaming black splendour among the celebrities around Turntable A.

Since the arrival of No. 2392 another mighty North Eastern freighter has joined them, one of Sir Vincent Raven's three-cylinder 'T3' 0-8-0s of the design first introduced in 1919, on loan from the National Railway Museum. For sheer hard slogging, with maximum-load mineral trains on steep gradients, I do not think these engines were ever surpassed on British metals. On seeing the 'P3s' next-door neighbour on Turntable A at York, the Great Western 2-8-0 No. 2818, I was reminded of a gladiatorial contest in weight pulling in 1921 initiated by the North British Railways on the formidable Glenfarg bank, when a Great Western 2-8-0 was tested against one of the then-new 'T3' three-cylinder 0-8-0s of the North Eastern, No. 903. The distance from Bridge of Earn to Glenfarg is 6.6 miles, and except for the first half-mile, which is level, the gradient is 1 in 75 throughout. The Great Western engine took a 590-ton load up in thirty-three minutes, start to stop, but on a

subsequent run with the load increased to 686 tons the engine slipped itself to a stand. The Swindon dry-sanding gear could not clear an accumulation of snow that was forming on the delivery pipe. The North Eastern engine, admittedly in better weather, made light of both load and gradient. She took a load of 703 tons up in exactly thirty minutes, and when the load was further increased to 755 tons the time was thirty-three minutes. The engine was working literally 'all out' for most of the way, and no difficulty was found in maintaining full boiler pressure throughout. If at some future time the preserved 'T3' pays a courtesy visit to York she should surely be positioned next to her old rival. The preserved engine still retains her B R number 63460, but she is actually the very first 'T3' No. 901.

The North Yorkshire Moors Railway is honoured in having two very celebrated members of the numerous Stanier 'Black Five' 4-6-0 family on its strength. There is the standard version, represented by No. 5428 *Eric Treacy,* and the unique 4767 built by the L M S in H. G. Ivatt's time, having Stephenson link motion, and named appropriately *George Stephenson.* No words of mine are necessary to extol the part that Bishop Treacy played in the furthering of the railway enthusiast interest, so skilfully blended with his great work as a churchman. It is fitting that one of the two locomotives named after him should be allocated to a preserved line in the county wherein the greatest of his life's work was performed. The 'Black Five' with Stephenson's link motion, when in ordinary service, had the reputation of being the strongest engine of all in getting away from rest and in mounting a heavy bank with a big load — altogether another ideal engine for that fearsome gradient up to Goathland.

On 5 May 1979, I was invited to join in a threefold celebration on the North Yorkshire Moors Railway. For some years the line had in its keeping an interesting example of Great Northern locomotive practice in the earliest Ivatt period, in the handsome saddle tank 0-6-0 No. 1247, the private property of Captain W. G. Smith. So far as

The restored N E R 'P3' class 0-6-0 No. 2392 climbing the gradient past Beck Holes on the run from Grosmont to Goathland, May 1974   *David Eatwell*

The wild moorland scenery around Goathland is typified in this shot of a train climbing the gradient, hauled by 'Black Five' 4-6-0 No. 5428 *Eric Treacy*, August 1975
David Eatwell

the machinery was concerned this engine was of Stirling design, but forty-five engines built between 1897 and 1899 had boilers of Ivatt's standard pattern with a dome and his own neat casing over the Ramsbottom safety valves. Engine No. 1247 was one of batch of twenty-five built in 1899 by Sharp, Stewart & Co. and numbered 1226 to 1250. Thus, in 1979, the engine was eighty years old. She had also been in private ownership for twenty years, and indeed one of her first expeditions after restoration was to work an excursion from London to the Bluebell line. The third anniversary celebrated on 5 May was the seventieth birthday of the Stephenson Loco-

motive Society, the Tees-side branch of which has been such a strong supporter of both the North Yorkshire Moors Railway and the North Eastern Locomotive Preservation Group.

It was a happy gathering that day in a former Great Western saloon that was attached to a train No. 1247 worked from Grosmont to Pickering and back, though the weather, with snow on the high moors, was anything but seasonable. The engine sheds at Grosmont, which provide shelter for no fewer than seventeen locomotives are located on the south side of the tunnel which replaced the original single-tracked small bore 'hole' built when traction on the Whitby and Pickering Railway was by horse. The hole is still there, an intriguing piece of industrial archaeology (!), and through it the shed staff and their privileged visitors make their way between the sheds and the passenger station. A notable engine on shed was an ex-L N E R class 'Kl' 2-6-0 No. 2005, handsomely repainted in the apple-green livery. This class originated from Edward Thompson's rebuilding of one of the West Highland 'K4' three-cylinder 2-6-0s of Sir Nigel Gresley. One of our party at lunch in the saloon that day was Peter Townend, formerly shedmaster at Kings Cross Top Shed, whom, as we both recalled that day, I first met on the footplate of a 'K4' on the West Highland line.

No ex-Great Western tender locomotives are at present attached to the North Yorkshire Moors Railway, but the Southern is nobly represented by one of R. E. L. Maunsell's 'S15' class mixed traffic 4-6-0s. Engine No. 841, recently named *Greene King*, is one of the very last batches of locomotives built for the Southern under Maunsell's direction. The design itself dates from 1927 and was an exact mixed-traffic counterpart of the 'King Arthur', with an interchangeable front-end. Although designated 'S15' for traffic purposes, the design differs in some important respects from the original Urie 'S15' of the London and South Western Railway in having smaller cylinders and a higher boiler pressure, together with long-lap, long-travel valves. One of the Urie 'S15s', No. 506, has also been preserved, and is on the Winchester and Alton Railway.

The association of the railway with the North York Moors National Park is providing a useful additional traffic. The line crosses high moorland, much of which is far from any highways, and from headquarters at Pickering station scenic runs are operated. For this service diesel railcars are used, to give the maximum outlook from picture windows. The service caters more for the ordinary holiday maker in the district than for the railway enthusiast, who would naturally prefer to be hauled by a vintage steam locomotive. Nevertheless a front seat in the diesel railbus gives a superb view of the line itself, with all its twistings and turnings, and can give a greater appreciation of the problems that were involved in the construction of the line. In his fascinating *Highways and Byways in Yorkshire*, Arthur H. Norway refers to the countryside as '. . . this towering wilderness of moors and crags stretching from the very sea coast into lands so solitary that only the curlews know their intricacies'.

Pickering itself was, strangely enough, a *Lancastrian* stronghold in the Wars of the Roses. But to quote Norway again, writing of the Castle:

One small square tower is fairly perfect yet; but if I look down on it and try to reconstruct the aspect of the place as the Second Richard saw it when he came riding up the hill a captive, wondering only whether it was here that the release would reach him from a world which had lost its savour, suddenly the outlines of the past are sent swimming into fragments like the reflections in a pool when a stone is cast into it, and I am called back rudely to the present unromantic age by the sight and sound of shunting trains just below the Castle wall. To what purpose should I listen for whispers out of the fourteenth century when the loud rattle of the nineteenth fills the air?

Unfortunately he did not know whether it was a long-boilered goods or a Fletcher 'BTP' that was causing the disturbance! The moors can be magnificent, especially in the late summer when the heather is in full bloom; but I have known the line also when the whole prospect was shrouded in rain clouds so low as to give the impression of dense fog.

The North Yorkshire Moors is primarily a steam railway, but in addition to the rail bus they have other diesel locomotives, including a really big diesel hydraulic from the Western Region, the *Western Lady*. Gradients of 1 in 49 were nothing

new to a locomotive that took the Cornish Riviera Express over the mountains of the South Devon line; and such a locomotive could be highly effective in hauling really heavy loads in the tourist season. The North Yorkshire Moors Railway, although building up a tradition that has developed from its historic associations with the Whitby and Pickering Railway, has become a gathering ground for locomotives of many origins, and in addition to the 'Westerns' they have one of the South Wales 0-6-2 tanks, designed in Collett's time at Swindon to provide a standard replacement unit for the many different varieties of tank engines in service up to 1922 on the various amalgamated and absorbed railways in South Wales from the time of the grouping. This preserved engine is No. 6619, built in 1928.

The line itself is the longest of all the private standard gauge railways in this country; and while one can rejoice that it is not completely isolated from B R, as are some of the others, the connection at Grosmont with the inland route from Middlesbrough to Whitby is rather like that of the back door. When B R closed the direct line from Grosmont to the south I do not suppose that any of the bureaucrats involved ever envisaged that part of that bleak, windswept line over the moors would be opened again. In fact the breach at the southern end is less than six miles long, from Pickering to the one-time Rillington Junction on the York-Scarborough line. Now that British Railways themselves are running steam specials and the Scarborough line is one of the prescribed routes, could we look forward to a time when that six miles between Rillington and Pickering could be restored? What a magnificent route it would be for steam-hauled specials, from Leeds or York, or even further afield, to Whitby!

Climbing the 1 in 49 gradient past Beck Holes, a heavily loaded charter special is hauled by the 0-6-2 Lambton Colliery tank engine No. 29 and banked in rear by ex-N E R 'P3' class 0-6-0 No. 2392, April 1973
David Eatwell

THE GREAT CENTRAL

When its dour and humourless Chairman, Sir Edward Watkin, persuaded the Manchester, Sheffield and Lincolnshire Railway to embark on its bitterly opposed London extension, to construct a splendid high speed main line from its hitherto most southerly point at Annesley in the Nottinghamshire coalfield area to link up with the Metropolitan Railway (of which he was also Chairman) at Quainton Road, it became a veritable 'Ishmael' of railways. It was vigorously opposed, particularly by two of the largest and most wealthy lines in the country, the Midland and the London and North Western. It changed its name to Great Central, and adopted the motto FORWARD; but the latter might instead have been: '. . . *de l'audace, et encore de l'audace, et toujours de l'audace!'* Although Sir Edward Watkin did not remain in office to see the project through, his successors brought the new line into operation in a spirit of boundless enterprise. In every detail the railway was immaculate and most carefully thought out. Its progress was tremendous; but the traffic did not come, and financially, if not exactly a dead loss, it did no more than pay its way. The shareholders got practically nothing.

Yet travelling on the Great Central was a delight, not only to railway enthusiasts but to the relatively few who forsook the London and North Western, or the Midland, to travel north from Marylebone. At the time of grouping when it was merged with the Great Northern, the North Eastern and the Great Eastern, its lack of profitability was balanced by the continued success of others, and in the difficult days of the 1930s it kept going with much of its original *élan*. In World War II it had the honour of taking Sir Winston Churchill on the first stage of his journey north to the Atlantic Meeting with President Roosevelt in 1941. After the war its equipment and rolling stock were very much run down, and in such a systematic analysis of profitability, or otherwise, as undertaken in the Beeching era no case could be made for its retention. But in the railway enthusiast world the Great Central had never lacked supporters, and when the threat of closure for the whole of the line that had been newly enterprised in 1899 became more than an alarming rumour, its friends got together to launch a preservation movement that has had no parallel elsewhere.

After all, this was not the closure of some branch or a redundant cross-country connection; this was a main line, and any preservation scheme must bear this in mind. It was *'de l'audace'* all over again. With a centre of activity based on Loughborough the earliest proposals involved purchasing the section of line between Ruddington in the north and the approach to Leicester at Abbey Lane Sidings. The distance was nearly nineteen miles, a stretch that the fast trains of old covered in as many minutes, or a little less. Among the optimistic launchers of the scheme there were some who felt this was no case for a 'light railway'. This was to be a 'main line' in very truth, with express speed running — no dawdling at 25 mph on the Great Central! The more prudent spirits realized, however, that such high hopes were out of place, and that a much more modest beginning was the only practical way. Nevertheless the words 'main line' were not dropped, and the Main Line

Steam Trust Ltd was formed to get the project under way. Arrangements were made to lease the section of line between Loughborough and Rothley, five and a half miles, and a Light Railway Order was obtained.

The Great Central in 1974; what the approach to Loughborough looked like when partial restoration began! A train for Quorn, hauled by the Manning-Wardle 0-6-0T locomotive *Littleton*, is leaving
Brian Morrison

I hope the enthusiasts who are backing the Great Central Main Line project will not take my next few paragraphs too hardly. Let there be no doubt about this: from 1921 when I first encountered it there has been no keener Great Central enthusiast than me. In my early train logging days when my parents' home was at Barrow-in-Furness, and I used to go there from London at bank holiday weekends, I gladly endured a chain of semi-fast trains through the night following a fast and exhilarating run down to Sheffield on the 6.20 p.m. from Marylebone. I astonished the parents of a school friend by insisting on travelling from Sheffield to London by Great Central instead of by Midland. I saw the Great Central in very many aspects, and all I saw was good — nay, magnificent. Yet somehow, from its very inception, I could not be enthusiastic about the preservation scheme centred at Loughborough.

It was in the centre of what had been a very fast stretch of line. The down expresses were allowed twenty-five minutes to cover the 23.4 miles from Leicester to Nottingham, while the early morning newspaper flyer was allowed only twenty-two minutes to the stop at Nottingham, Arkwright Street. On six successive runs of my own the speeds passing through Loughborough were 81, 78, 79½, 83½, 80½ and 80½ mph. At the outset of the preservation scheme I think there were some who hoped that once the track was rehabilitated they might be able to 'let rip' as of old; but the revived Great Central became something unique among the preserved railways. All the other major projects concerned branch lines, or steeply graded secondary routes on which the 25 mph limit, the maximum under 'light railway' conditions, was not greatly different from the speeds run when the lines were under their original ownership; but over such a one-time speedway as the Great Central the circumstances of revival were rather sad. Never-

The restored 4-4-0 express locomotive No. 506 *Butler Henderson* on exhibition at Loughborough, September 1976
                                            Brian Morrison

theless, a brave attempt has been made to put on a show, and a rare collection of locomotives of all shapes, sizes and vintages have been assembled or have their home base at Loughborough.

The only true Great Central engine is the 4-4-0 'Director' class No. 506 *Butler Henderson,* built at Gorton in 1919. It is on loan from the National Railway Museum and is at present for exhibition only. No. 506 was the first of the so-called 'Improved Director' class, though so far as actual performance on the line I, and most other recorders, could discern little if any difference between the work of the original ten, numbered from 429 to 438, and the later ones. The only appreciable difference, apart from the purely superficial one that the later engines had side-windowed cabs, was they also had a considerably *reduced* heating surface in the superheaters. But both varieties were extremely fast and powerful engines, frequently reaching speeds of 90 mph on the longer downhill stretches of the main line south of Leicester. Both varieties came in for attention from outside the G C R. During World War I the original series was featured in a long and highly laudatory article in the American technical journal *Railway Mechanical Engineer,* under the title 'An English Eight-Wheeled Locomotive', while the improved version was chosen after grouping as a new standard class for the Scottish Area, and twenty-four were built by private firms. Originally unnamed, they were later named after characters in the Waverley novels.

After World War II engines of the Thompson 'B1' were extensively used on the Great Central line, though on schedules that were considerably slower. Two of them—one, No. 61264, still carrying its B R number, and No. 1306 *Mayflower*—are based at Loughborough, the latter beautifully turned out in L N E R apple green. The 'B1s' were notable as a skilful wartime synthesis of existing basic parts that produced a good mixed traffic 4-6-0 without involving any capital expenditure on new tools, patterns and so on. The boiler was that of the 'Sandringham' class; the 6 ft 2 in. coupled wheels were those of the 'V2'

Green Arrow 2-6-2; and the cylinders were those of the 'K2' 2-6-0. It produced a class that was very much needed at the time. Sir Nigel Gresley had designed his prototype 'V4' 2-6-2 *Bantam Cock* for this particular function, but it was a design that included too many refinements to be a good proposition for wartime and the years of austerity that followed.

As traffic machines the 'B1s' were rather rough, unsophisticated workhorses, harsh and tiring to ride, as I found on a number of lengthy footplate journeys, but they did the job, and were as economical as any engines of their particular power class. During the celebrated Interchange Trials of 1948, organized by the Railway Executive soon after nationalization, one of the test routes for the mixed traffic locomotives was from Marylebone to Manchester; and it is of great interest that the locomotives now gathered at Loughborough include examples of all four designs that worked through under test conditions in 1948. In addition to the 'B1', which represented the L N E R, there are now an L M S 'Black Five' 4-6-0, a Southern 'West Country' Pacific, and the actual Great Western 'Hall' that ran in the trials, No. 6990 *Witherslack Hall.* For the record the actual engines involved, and those now at Loughborough are:

Railway	GWR	LMS	LNER	Southern
Tested in 1948	6990	5253	61163	34006
Now at Loughborough	6990	5231	61264 1306	34039

In passing, I wonder how many people know where Witherslack Hall is, and anything of its romantic history? By the time the G W R had got 290 Halls they were casting their net far beyond Great Western territory for more names. Witherslack lies just to the north of the A590 road from Levens Bridge to Grange-over-Sands. In my early days of photography on the London and North Western Railway north of Oxenholme, I used to pass near to it when cycling from Barrow.

The present mansion was built in 1871 for the 16th Earl of Derby, but it stands on the site of a manor house dating back to Plantagenet times. At the end of the Wars of the Roses Henry VII dispossessed the current owner, who had been on the Yorkist side, and gave it to Sir Thomas Broughton; but a year later, when the Pretender, Lambert Simnell, landed at Piel with an army of Irish and German mercenaries intending to seize back the throne for the Yorkists, Broughton showed so little gratitude to his king that he joined the rebels, and marched south with them! After their defeat at Newark, Broughton managed to escape, and got back to Witherslack where, to avoid capture and almost certain execution, he lived *incognito* among his tenants until his death in old age.

Engine No. 6990 is owned by the Witherslack Hall Locomotive Society, and 61264 by the Thompson B1 Locomotive Society. In 1948 the trains all stopped at Loughborough and were considerably slower than the fastest trains of the inter-war period, although the down train had a sharp allowance of only twelve minutes, start to stop, for the 9.8 miles from Leicester to Loughborough. Not all the competing engines kept that time. The Southern engine, in 1948, was named *Bude,* and the engine now preserved at Loughborough is *Boscastle.*

I must admit to a liking for named engines — with certain very definite reservations. In one of his now historic articles on 'Locomotive and Train Working in the Latter Part of the Nineteenth Century' Ahrons poked fun at the practice of the Brighton Railway in naming its local tank engines after obscure villages on the line, although instancing *Crawley* as a very suitable name for many of the services of the L B & S C R! But to my way of thinking a name should be good, as a name, as well as appropriate in other respects, and I would suggest that the practice has sunk to rock bottom on the 'Black Five' 4-6-0 now working on the Great Central line.

In 1927 I thought that the naming of the new three-cylinder 4-6-0s of the L M S after famous regiments was an inspiration, so cleverly combining on the class leader the name of a great regiment with the conception of locomotives hauling the crack Anglo-Scottish expresses on the Royal Mail route. The 'Royal Scot' train was so splendid a counterpart to the East Coast 'Flying Scotsman'. The first twenty-six engines of the 'Royal Scot' class had really first rate names. It was when it was desired to honour other regiments, and the names of historic locomotives allocated to engines 6126 and 6149 began to be superseded, that the rot set in. *Vesta,* an engine with which I had particular associations, got renamed *The Prince of Wales's Volunteers, South Lancashire.* This was not among the worst; but one could not have the same attachment to such a cumbersome title, and I am afraid that after the change I found solace in referring to the engine as '6137'. It was much cosier.

The Great Central itself went a bit mad in the earlier days of the London extension when one of the beautiful Robinson 'Atlantics' was named *The Rt. Hon. Viscount Cross, GCB, GCSI.* A wag once suggested that the initials GCB and GCSI stood for secret offices within the Great Central Railway organization. The long and unduly grandiose title was carried by one of the four three-cylinder compound 'Atlantics', all of which were named. After the introduction of the 'Sandringham' class 4-6-0s at Leicester shed in 1936, all four compound 4-4-2s were transferred to Immingham. Fortunately when the 'Director' class 4-4-0s were introduced in 1913, and all ten locomotives were named after members of the Board, the titles put on were as commendably brief as they were euphonious. *Charles Stuart-Wortley,* for example, was a great deal better than The Right Hon. Charles B. Stuart-Wortley, KC, MP, which was the full title of the gentleman concerned. *Worsley-Taylor,* an engine of the class for which I retain a special regard, had an even briefer rendering of its name. But to return to that 'Black Five' of today, even my poor old '6137' of the 'Royal Scot' class cannot, I think, hold a candle to *3rd (Volunteer) Batallion The Worcestershire and Sherwood*

A transformation in track: the Great Central line near Quorn, in September 1976, with only one line in use. A southbound train hauled by ex-L M S 'Black Five'

4-6-0 No. 5231 named *3rd (Volunteer) Battalion, The Worcestershire and Sherwood Foresters Regiment*

Brian Morrison

Foresters Regiment! Let us instead refer to the overloaded engine as 5231.

Turning for a moment from locomotives to coaching stock, and consideration for the inner man: when the Great Central opened its London extension in 1899 it was its proud boast that every express train was vestibuled throughout and carried a refreshment car. Although there were never many such trains on the line, the fact that *every* express train was so equipped was an almost sensational innovation in 1899. After all, in the early 1900s the Great Western had only one restaurant car in each direction on its London-Birmingham-Wolverhampton service, which they ran via Oxford. The Great Central's further service was that one could obtain hot meals from the grill at any time of day, and that it was only on late evening trains like the 6.20 p.m. Marylebone to Bradford that meals were confined to a full *table d'hôte* dinner. The Main Line Steam Trust, operating the five and a half mile length of the Great Central, is continuing in this audaciously enterprising tradition by running a Gresley buffet car on all its trains, by serving lunches on midday trains at weekends, and running dinner trains on alternate Saturday nights in summer. This is a rather astonishing attraction on trains that travel such a short distance, and do not exceed 25 mph.

The Norwegian 2-6-0 No. 377 *King Haakon VII* at Loughborough, September 1974   *Brian Morrison*

Reverting to locomotives, a machine of unusual and great historic interest now at Loughborough is the light Norwegian 2-6-0 No. 377, now named *King Haakon VII*. This is one of a class of forty-five, of which there were originally five minor varieties, designed in the first place for operating over lightly laid track on the branch lines. They have been likened in their capacity and use to the British 2-6-0 engines of class '2' derived from the Ivatt design of the L M S, in 1947. But the engine now working from Loughborough has a special interest: in 1940, when the Germans invaded Norway, No. 377 was used to haul the coach in which King Haakon was conveyed north to meet the warship which brought him to Britain. The engine, which was built in 1919, was purchased for display at Bressingham Steam Museum, near Diss, Norfolk, and arrived there in 1970. It makes a picturesque addition to the stud at Loughborough.

It unfortunately attained some unwanted publicity in 1976, through involvement in an accident, luckily not fatal, which provided a salutary lesson to all who are running private steam railways with volunteer labour. In earlier chapters of this book the importance was stressed of keeping the boilers of preserved steam locomotives in serviceable condition up to a standard acceptable to the Railway Inspectorate of the Ministry of Transport; and that means carrying out hydraulic and steaming tests under the supervision of accredited engineering surveyors of established insurance companies, fully experienced with boiler work. What happened on 7 March 1976 was that one of two fusible plugs on the firebox crown of the *King Haakon VII* was blown out of place into the fire. Steam at 170 lb per sq. in. escaped into the firebox, blew open the firehole door, allowing scalding steam and burning coals to sweep out on to the footplate. All four volunteer enginemen were scalded in varying degrees of severity. The driver was the least injured, and managed to apply the brakes to bring the train to rest before jumping for safety. There were 200 passengers in the train, but none was injured.

The cause of this alarming accident, which might have had disastrous results had the driver been so incapacitated as to be unable to apply the brakes, was the incorrect fitting of two fusible plugs in the firebox crown. Both had tapered threads that did not match the taper of the holes into which they were inserted. This meant that when the top threads of the plugs were tight in the holes the bottom threads had some clearance, and the plugs were holding only by a few threads. The unfortunate volunteer fitter who did this work was not sufficiently experienced to realize the danger inherent in what he had done. One hopes that the account of the accident given in the *Railway Magazine* will have been read as so many letters of fire by every private administration operating steam locomotives.

The course of events on the *King Haakon VII* was as follows: in April 1975 the engine was being retubed. The engineering surveyor examining the boiler asked for the two fusible plugs to be removed, so that they, and the holes in the crown plate, could be examined. This was not done at the time, and a week later when he examined the boiler a second time new plugs had been fitted. He did not ask for their removal for inspection in the belief that the work had been done by an experienced boilersmith. The surveyor instead asked for a hydraulic test, at 230 lb per sq. in., considerably above the working pressure of the boiler, and when this proved satisfactory he issued the appropriate certificate. Just over a fortnight later the boiler was given a steam test in the surveyor's presence, which it also passed satisfactorily. The engine was subsequently returned to traffic, and ten months later the accident occurred.

The question of boiler examination on volunteer railways, as highlighted by this accident, is seen to have acquired an aspect very different from that existing in the steam days of British Railways. I am not suggesting that the circumstances apply generally — indeed I know they do not in many cases; but on the private railways insurance surveyors have been employed 'who are experienced in high-pressure marine steam work, but are often as ignorant as their clients of locomotive boilers', to quote the *Railway Magazine*. To those who have never ridden on the footplate on a steam locomotive, and especially when working at normal express speed, the extent to which *vibration* plays a part in the ordinary run of things will not be appreciated; and while those badly fitted plugs on the *King Haakon VII* might have held fast in stationary conditions for the full period between successive boiler examinations, in locomotive working, even on the leisurely Great Central line of today, the normal progress could, and did, rattle one of them loose.

One of the latest locomotives destined for Loughborough, but at the time of writing not yet arrived, is the very last express passenger steam engine built for service on British Railways, the class 8 three-cylinder 4-6-2 No. 71000 *Duke of Gloucester*. I wish I could be more enthusiastic about this engine. I saw it first at Crewe in 1954 on the occasion of a visit by the Institution of Locomotive Engineers, when the engine was brand new. It was very much the 'baby' of J. F. Harrison, who was then Chief Mechanical Engineer of the London Midland Region. He was an L N E R man by training, and still very much so by sentiment; and I shall always remember a remark he made when emphasizing to me some points in the design of No. 71000: 'I think Sir Nigel Gresley would approve'. On reflection I am not sure that he would have done! The engine had a boiler like that of the 'Britannias', but the valve gear was the Caprotti, and although it gave all the freedom in running characteristic of that gear I wonder if in the light of his experience with the 2-8-2 engine *Cock o' the North,* and its subsequent conversion to piston valves, Gresley would have put any form of poppet valves on No. 71000.

However, it was not the valve gear that earned for the engine its somewhat shaky reputation, but its insatiable appetite for coal. I was privileged to witness at first hand from the dynamometer car, some of the full-dress trials conducted on the stationary plant at Swindon, and it was evident that the draughting needed some special examination and adjustment. As delivered for testing the maximum steaming rate was less than that of a Great Western 'King', and considerably less than that of a 'Britannia', even though No. 71000 had a twin-orifice blastpipe and double-chimney. The Swindon testing staff wished to keep the engine longer so that experiments could be made to improve the draughting, but it was wanted back on the L M Region, and took up regular work in the 'Pacific' link at Crewe North Shed. The coal consumption was much heavier than that of the 'Stanier' 4-6-2s, and for this reason the engine did not work on the longer turns, such as Crewe to Perth, or Crewe to Glasgow. I gathered No. 71000 was not a very popular engine.

The restoration of the engine by The Duke of Gloucester Steam Locomotive Trust is nevertheless significant of the interest naturally centred upon it as the last of its kind, and when the work is finished, and it enters passenger service at Loughborough the duties on the present Great Central line will not tax the steaming capacity. There is little doubt that the large firegrate will involve a substantial coal consumption, for the simple reason that, when steaming, coal has to be used to keep the firebars covered, however thinly.

Taken all round, the Great Central line of today has some very interesting locomotive associations, in the bringing together of examples of all four contestants in the mixed traffic 1948 trials; in the historic *King Haakon VII;* and especially in having the only surviving Great Central express locomotive. There is always the prospect of eating a *table d' hôte* lunch, hauled by *Butler Henderson* at a speed not exceeding 25 mph.

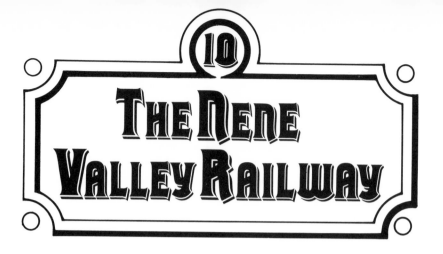

THE NENE VALLEY RAILWAY

The City of Peterborough used to be a great railway centre. Even in pre-grouping days there were not many provincial cities of its size where the trains of no fewer than five separate companies could be seen, all hauled by their own engines. The Great Northern and the Great Eastern were 'naturals', by virtue of geography; so, by a stretch of south-westerly enterprise, came the Midland and Great Northern Joint. But the Midland was there on its own metals, while the London and North Western, through one of the oldest of its constituents, the London and Birmingham, was actually the first to enterprise a branch line to the city, from Blisworth, via Northampton, in June 1845. The Midland arrived from Leicester in October 1846, and the Eastern Counties, later Great Eastern, from Ely in January 1847. These three all joined forces at what afterwards became known as Peterborough East. The Great Northern, the most important of the trunk lines, was the last to arrive, with the Lincolnshire loop line from Boston completed in October 1848, and the main line to London in August 1850. The layout and ownership of the various lines can be seen from the accompanying map, showing the situation at the time of grouping in 1923.

At this stage, and in view of recent trends, I cannot resist quoting a piece from an old book of 1851 entitled *Rides on Railways* by one Samuel Sidney. He refers to Peterborough as '. . . a city without population, without manufacturers, without trade, without a good inn, or even a copy of *The Times*, except at the railway station; a city which would have gone on slumbering to the present hour without a go-ahead principle of any kind, and which has, nevertheless, by the accident of situation, had railway greatness thrust upon it in the most extraordinary manner. The Cathedral viewed, nothing remains to detain the traveller in this peculiarly stupid city!' Anyone knowing Peterborough today, and its many-sided activities, quite apart from the glories of one of the most distinctive and romantic of all our English cathedrals, can smile at the comments of this singularly unperceptive scribe of 130 years ago; though of course there is no doubt that railways, and particularly the Great Northern, played no small part in revitalizing the city. And it was the rather misplaced enterprise of the Great Northern, in its nineteenth-century antagonism towards the Midland, that laid the foundation on which one of the most interesting of the private railways of today has been built.

Two cross-country branches of the London and North Western Railway, one from Rugby, and one already mentioned, from Blisworth and Northampton, converged at Yarwell Junction, about eight miles from Peterborough, where just

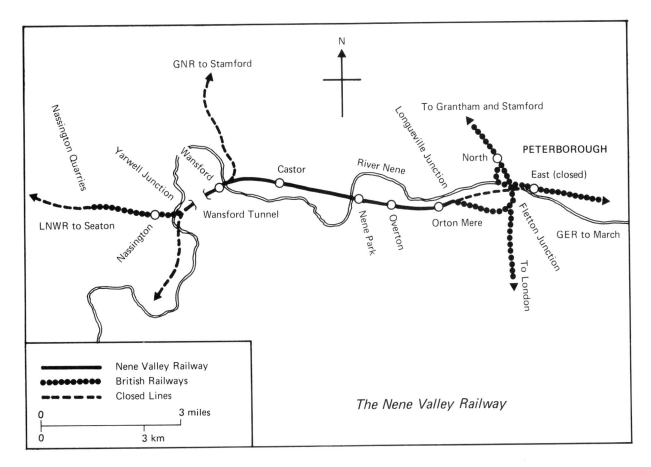

short of the East Station an end-on junction was made with the Great Eastern Railway. The Midland line that ran alongside the East Coast main and then veered westward to Stamford, continued on a somewhat circuitous course through Oakham and Melton Mowbray to join the main line at Syston, and so into Leicester. The Great Northern may not have seen eye-to-eye with the London and North Western on many issues; but when it was a case of 'wiping the eye' of the Midland they were whole-heartedly unanimous. And so it was between Peterborough and Leicester. The G N R obtained running powers over twenty-four and three-quarter miles of the L N W line from Peterborough to Drayton Junction; joint ownership was arranged over twelve and a quarter miles to Marefield South Junction, leaving the Great Northern only twelve miles of new line to construct, which they consummated with a handsome, though unnecessarily large, terminal station in Leicester.

A short length of the new construction was at Peterborough itself. Although the service initiated in 1883 was one of no more than four trains a day in each direction, stopping at all intermediate stations, they started from the North rather than the East station, and to make connection a short link was made from Fletton Junction, on the main line one and a half miles south of the North station, curving round through a full right angle to join the L N W R line at Longueville Junction. The Great Northern service between Peterborough and Leicester was a dead loss, and it was abandoned in 1916. The junction at Longueville was removed,

99

and the line from Fletton Junction used only to provide access to some industrial sidings; it could hardly have been imagined then that circumstances sixty years later would require the relaying of the junction at Longueville, and by volunteer labour into the bargain. How the Nene Valley Railway came about is as fascinating a story as any in the history of private railway preservation.

The sequence of events, from 1968, was entirely different from that of any other preserved railway, and in every respect, too, the line has remained different. It began with the purchase from British Railways of a class '5' mixed traffic 4-6-0 No. 73050, by the Rev. Richard Paton. He intended that, named *City of Peterborough*, it should be preserved on a plinth as a reminder of the City's railway heritage — shades of Mr Samuel Sidney — but the engine arrived from Patricroft shed, Manchester, under her own steam and in such relatively good condition that the reverend gentleman and his friends decided to restore the engine to full working order, with a view to running trips from Peterborough. A locomotive society was formed to further this particular interest. The engine in question was one of the British Railways standard version of the famous L M S 'Black Five', and had been built in 1954.

At the beginning of 1968 the prospects for railway enthusiasts in Great Britain were gloomy in two ways. It was fairly certain that before the year was out steam traction would have ceased on British Railways and that the death knell would have been sounded for the Museum of British Transport at Clapham. The British Railways Board was unwilling to carry the incubus of the continuing and increasing financial loss on its staffing and maintenance, and sought to dispose of its collection of relics. At first the Minister of State, Department of Education and Science, seemed able to think only of an enlargement of the existing railway museum at York. However, a suggestion was put forward for an alternative site at Peterborough, where the closing of the East Station would afford some space and where the advantage of rail connection existed, which the museum at Clapham never had. That the government decided to house the railway collection in an outpost of the Science Museum at York, and on a scale and with a magnificence that none of us could have dared hope for in 1968, is a matter of history; but the suggestion that the site might be at Peterborough sparked off local interest.

Far from 'slumbering . . . without a go-ahead principle of any kind', as averred by Samuel Sidney, the Peterborough City Council, in providing for the needs of its greatly expanding population, had decided upon the development of the six-mile-long Nene Park as a leisure centre; and a feasibility study was made of the prospects of a Nene Valley steam railway using the former London and North Western line through the park from the site of Longueville Junction to Wansford, five and a half miles. The proposals were finalized in 1972 and, to the delight of the railway society, accepted by the City Council. In the following year the Peterborough Development Corporation purchased the section of track concerned, together with sidings and run-round facilities at each end, and leased them to the Peterborough Railway Society Ltd. The society had in the meantime been fully reconstituted as a company limited by guarantee and registered as a charity. This was a very important development in the history of railway preservation in that the project had been embarked upon with the co-operation and financial backing of a major local authority, to provide an educational and recreational amenity in their district.

When it was first made available to the Peterborough Railway Society, the Nene Valley was isolated from the British Railways system. At its western end permanent way along the old line to Rugby existed only as far as Nassington Quarries, and although the connection at Longueville Junction had been briefly restored after World War II the track had been lifted again in the 1950s. The inconvenience of having to transport rolling stock by road to the new line was considered too great, and in March 1974, with the ready agreement of British Railways, the railway society's own volunteer engineers re-made the connection at Longueville Junction, linking up the new Nene Valley Railway with the one-time Great Northern branch to Fletton Junction. The route of the Peterborough-Leicester passenger service was thereby restored, at any rate to the extent of Nene Valley operation.

Before restoration of the track and lineside equipment had advanced to the stage of enabling trains to run, the locomotives and rolling stock were stored at a sugarbeet factory of the British Sugar Corporation, served by the connecting line from Fletton Junction. One of the units so ensconced was the ex-B R '5MT' 4-6-0 No. 73050 *City of Peterborough*, to which the coat of arms of the city had already been applied below the number on the cab side. Late in 1972, at the factory, there was an explosion in the combustion chamber of one of the factory's boilers, which temporarily interrupted production. But three days later, and before things had been seriously affected, engine No. 73050 was lit up, steamed and connected to the works steam line. This unusual 'industrial' boiler was steamed continuously for eight days, and kept production going while emergency repairs were carried out to the regular boiler. The Peterborough Railway Society was glad of this opportunity to help out, and help repay the British Sugar Corporation for their hospitality in housing the locomotive for more than two years.

It was at about this same time that the Nene Valley Railway was asked if it would like to have one or two Swedish class 'S1' 2-6-4 tank engines that had been privately purchased. It was an attractive offer; but of course with any Continental locomotive or rolling stock there could be problems with side and overhead clearance. This question had to be settled, and here the Peterborough Railway Society had a stroke of luck. The followers of Philip Shirley, in furthering his policy of tearing down anything that had been remotely connected with steam, had stripped the line of many lineside fixtures that would have encroached upon the loading gauge limits to which Continental

locomotives and rolling stock comply. A careful examination revealed that only one short station platform and one private road overbridge infringed the limits. But there was another consideration that had to be taken into account. If platforms for the stations in the Nene Park were to be built to accommodate the Continental loading gauge, a difficulty would arise on trains of British coaching stock, because there would be an unacceptable gap between the footboards and platforms which would have to be overcome by fitting extended footboards to British stock.

It was a difficult decision for a newly formed railway society to have to make. If the Continental loading gauge were adopted, there would be difficulties in running through excursion trains to the Nene Valley line from other parts of British Railways, because although standard coaching stock could be conveyed round the connecting link between the Fletton and Longueville junctions, in the interests of safety special arrangements would have to be made at the platforms to prevent passengers falling into the gap between carriage footboards and platform edges when alighting. On the other hand, if the more generous loading gauge were not adopted, the Swedish 2-6-4 tank engine offered, and any other Continental rolling stock, would have to remain static or severely constrained museum pieces, like the large express locomotives at Carnforth. The society took the commendable decision to adopt the Continental gauge, realizing that this gave them the unique opportunity of running Continental locomotives and rolling stock in Great Britain.

The Nene Valley Railway, as purchased by the Peterborough Development Corporation, extends from Longueville Junction to Yarwell Junction, with the final section from Wansford passing through a short tunnel. Restoration work had progressed far enough for the locomotives and rolling stock hitherto housed at the depot of the British Sugar Corporation to be moved to Wansford for display on two open days, on Easter Sunday and Monday 1974. Then the 4-6-0 *City of Peterborough* and the Swedish 2-6-4 tank were on

The Swedish 2-6-4T No. 1928 on display at Wansford Road station, August 1979. Note arrangements for car parking in the station yard   *Brian Morrison*

show, together with one of the ubiquitous Hunslet War Department saddle tank 0-6-0s, the *Jacks Green*, and two other industrial locomotives. The headquarters of the railway has been established at Wansford, which has been named a Steam Centre; but to me one of the most pleasing features of the enterprise is that the Society and railway should have as its headquarters such a beautiful example of a nineteenth-century country station building, in both size and architectural style.

It is interesting to hazard a guess at why the London and North Western Railway, not given to over indulgence in capital expenditure, should have built such a prestigious affair for what is, even now, little more than a village — albeit with a

major road junction one and a half miles away to the north. It was probably a district centre. The North Western made its ultimate arrival in Peterborough over the metals of the Great Eastern Railway, and Wansford lay just beyond the junction of the two lines from Rugby and Northampton. The station master could well have been the senior traffic department man in the area, and one to be looked after accordingly. The station buildings themselves have an identical architectural style to some of those on the Trent Valley section of the West Coast main line, which was built in 1847, two years after the line to Peterborough. In any event the Nene Valley Railway of today has in the station building at Wansford an architectural period piece of great charm and importance. In railway preservation projects I know there is a strong and quite natural tendency to emphasize the *steam* aspect; but Wansford has a little masterpiece in its station building. There is also a fine example of an L N W R signal box just beyond the level crossing.

To connoisseurs of locomotive practice, the decision of the Peterborough Railway Society to adopt the Continental loading gauge was

fortuitous beyond measure, because they have been able to have, in addition to a second Swedish tank engine and a fascinating little one from Denmark, an example of one of the most remarkable locomotive classes that ever ran the rails in Europe, the 'D' class 4-6-0 of the Nord. To many English visitors the 'D', introduced in 1901, was a general utility type, quite overshadowed in glamour and utilization by the famous de Glehn compound 'Atlantics', and in later years by successive designs of 'Pacific'; but in the design of

The Danish 0-6-0T No. 656 on train for Wansford, April 1980 *John Titlow*

the 'D' class, forced upon him indirectly by the strict limitation in axle loading insisted upon by the permanent way department of the Northern Railway, M. du Bousquet postulated a principle in design that was well ahead of the times. The compound 'Atlantics' were doing fine work on the fast boat trains between Paris, Boulogne and Calais, but the increasing loads, particularly of the intermediate express trains, made a six-coupled engine desirable. To save weight it was decided to use coupled wheels 5 ft 9 in. diameter, as on the previous mixed traffic 4-6-0s, instead of 6 ft 8 in. on the 'Atlantics', while retaining the same boiler as the Atlantics.

This resulted in a greater nominal tractive effort, but the French designers required a high speed express locomotive, and if the front end design was left unaltered the higher piston speeds due to the smaller coupled wheels would have involved internal losses from throttling. So the cross-sectional areas of the steam passages were increased by 25 per cent through the high pressure cylinders and by no less than 30 per cent through the low pressure. As a result, the new engines could develop the same tractive power at 75 mph as the previous 4-6-0 engines could at 60 mph. This was not all. After World War I when the Nord engineers were designing their new 'Super-Pacific' under the direction of M. Bréville, the cylinder design of the 1907 4-6-0s was taken as a guide, with equally beneficial results. The final development of the 4-6-0, which is to be seen in the locomotive now at work on the Nene Valley Railway, was the fitting in the 1930s of the Lemaître multiple-jet blastpipe, which further enhanced the performance. There were 125 engines of this class on the Northern Region of the SNCF. A very fine performance was recorded in 1938 in which a load of 440 tons was run over the 51.9 miles from Paris to Compiègne in fifty-two minutes, start to stop, and the ensuing 43.3 miles on to St Quentin

---

The Swedish 4-6-0 No. 1697 leaving Wansford for Orton Mere, tender first, September 1980   *John Titlow*

The de Glehn compound 4-6-0 from the Northern Railway of France running into the beautifully styled station of Wansford, during the filming of the BBC feature *Secret Army*, May 1978 *John Titlow*

covered in forty minutes. On level stretches of the line speed was sustained at the legal French maximum, then, of 74.5 mph.

It need hardly be added that no performance remotely approaching this could be expected, or allowed, on the Nene Valley Railway! But it is good to know that an engine belonging to a class with such an honourable record is to be seen running on English metals. She certainly has some interesting and appropriate Continental rolling stock to haul, which can be sampled on the run between Wansford and the new station at Orton Mere, near to Longueville Junction. One of the latest additions is a *Wagon Lit* dining car in which a full lunch service is provided. The car seats fifty-six passengers. I have not yet had an opportunity of sampling its gastronomical delights, but if meals are served with the pomp, circumstance and deliberation of a French restaurant car I should think that the meal would overlap the

return trip from Wansford to Orton Mere and back by quite a while. The single run of five and a half miles takes twenty minutes, and with a turn round time of ten minutes at Orton Mere, one is back at Wansford in fifty minutes from the start.

In addition to the French 4-6-0, the two Swedish tank engines and the little Danish 0-6-0, the Nene Valley Railway now has an interesting German 2-6-2 tank of the Bundesbahn '64' class. It is of a design introduced by the Reichsbahn in 1928, of which no fewer than 520 were built between then and 1940. Engine No. 064 − 305, which is at Peterborough, was built in 1936. Though efficient and popular machines in traffic, they could hardly be

106

termed very elegant, with so many fittings hung all over the outside. But it could certainly be claimed that everything was easily get-at-able! The same could not be said of one of the British express passenger locomotives now at Wansford, the Southern Railway 'Battle of Britain' class 4-6-2 *92 Squadron*. In producing his much publicized 'air smoothed' Pacifics of the 'Merchant Navy', 'West Country' and 'Battle of Britain' classes, O. V. S. Bulleid sought to make day-to-day maintenance unnecessary by encasing all the working parts, including the valve gear, in an oil bath. The whole exterior of the engine was enclosed in an air-smoothed casing, which led to the engines being nicknamed the 'spam-cans'. Although they were fast and powerful locomotives the enclosed valve motion, out of sight, sound, and smell, sometimes led to severe failures, and consequent delay in traffic.

The Nene Valley Railway received an unexpected bonus in recent times. The pioneer British Standard '7MT' 4-6-2 *Britannia* was normally allocated to the Severn Valley Railway, being the property of the Britannia Locomotive Society, but it was found unsuitable for that line and has since been transferred to Peterborough. In its way the *Britannia* is as significant and important an exhibit as the French class 'D' 4-6-0.

Quite apart from any political considerations, very few people in Britain viewed the nationalization of the railways in 1948 with equanimity. While some, crushed, infuriated or wearied by the rigours and uncertainties of civilian wartime travel, and without the slightest apprehension of the colossal service the railways of Britain had rendered towards the winning of the war, felt they were long overdue for new management, very many others, and not only railway enthusiasts, were sad at the thought that the individuality of the old companies was to disappear. But R. A. Riddles, the member of the new Railway Executive responsible for mechanical and electrical engineering, had a clear mandate to standardize motive power. It would have been so easy for him and his chosen lieutenants to have taken the well-tried

Stanier locomotives of the L M S that they knew so well and to have adapted them to national requirements. Instead they took the far more difficult course of assiduously studying the locomotive practice of the 'Big Four' of the grouping era, in order to incorporate their best features. Furthermore, they decided that the four main drawing offices, at Ashford, Derby, Doncaster and Swindon, should all have a share in the design of the new standard locomotives. The first of the new range, the class '7' 4-6-2, was named *Britannia* as befitted the class leader, and indeed the fleet leader, of the new era on the railways of Britain. That the new standard locomotives were not welcomed everywhere was perhaps inevitable, and they had not been in service very long before the great plan for the modernization of British Railways was launched, the most significant feature of which was to be the complete elimination of steam traction. But *Britannia* remains a milestone in British railway history. On the Nene Valley Railway she has been fitted with the Westinghouse air brake to haul the growing number of Continental coaches that are being assembled there.

The 4-6-0 locomotive *City of Peterborough* is also one of the range of British standard designs produced under Riddles's direction, though in that case it represented no more than a slight development from the L M S 'Black Five'. Although this engine came to the Nene Valley in a reasonably good state of repair, steam locomotives, even though lightly used, do not last for ever, and since her arrival in 1968 she has seen much service on the line. A link with the very early days of steam railways was forged when arrangements were made for her to be thoroughly overhauled by the firm of Peter Brotherhood Ltd, whose works are alongside the East Coast main line, a few miles north of Peterborough. This firm, long established in the field of agricultural machinery and the engines required for it, had not previously dealt with full-sized steam locomotives. But its founder, Peter Brotherhood, was one of the ten sons of that remarkable contractor, Brotherhood of Chippen-

ham, who among other things undertook 'the repair and maintenance of the earthwork and ballasting, the permanent way, sidings, station buildings, bridges and viaducts, tunnels and culverts, drains, level crossings, roads, fences and other works', on Brunel's main line of the Great Western, between Reading and Bristol, and over many branches as well. He also built locomotives in a factory beside the main line at Chippenham which is still intact, but now given over to the more usual Wiltshire industry of bacon curing.

A notable recent addition to the collection of Continental locomotives on the Nene Valley line is one of the big 'S' class 2-6-4 tanks of the Danish State Railways, first introduced in 1924. The engine now at Wansford was the last to be built and dates from 1928. The impressive appearance of this fine locomotive is to some extent impaired by the huge smoke-deflecting plates, which, added to the large side tanks, take away something of the grace which the fine proportions would give. But one must not quibble. It is good to have yet another notable Continental design on British metals.

One last thought for the enterprising group who are running the Nene Valley Railway: what about a London and North Western engine? Among the distinguished visitors that haul the trains back and forth through Nene Park it would be grand to have one representing the original builders and owners of the line. There are not many North Western engines in existence, but watching the Rainhill cavalcade and seeing that sprightly little 'Coal Tank' 0-6-2 No. 1054, built at Crewe in 1888, and now owned by the National Trust, the thought occurred to me — perhaps a little uncharitable to her present custodians — that she might be spirited away from relative seclusion at Dinting Steam Centre to run occasional trips over a real North Western route, though the pleasance of Nene Park.

Train of mixed Continental coaching stock hauled by the German 2-6-2T No. 64-305 and the Danish 0-6-0T, April 1980
John Titlow

STRATHSPEY

In my travels all over the world I do not think I have seen a finer prospect from a train than the view from the Highland Line descending from Carr Bridge to Aviemore. I am not forgetting breathtaking sights in the Canadian Rockies, or in the Blue Mountains of New South Wales, or even the prospect of Mount Shasta at dawn from the 'Coast Starlight' express of the Southern Pacific. It is the magnificent grouping of the mountains, the interplay of light and shade revealing the immense clefts between the peaks, that makes such a stupendous backdrop to the Spey Valley. Beside the river runs the only steam railway now regularly operating in the Highlands of Scotland. As befits a railway in such a setting there is a wealth of history behind the five and a quarter miles of line between Aviemore and Boat of Garten.

The Highland Railway was an entirely indigenous enterprise. Here were no barons of industry striving to cash in on the mania for railway promoting that led to such a wild and catastrophic spending spree in England. The Highland chieftains and the burghers of Inverness wanted a railway through to Perth, and these commissioned their fellow townsman, the eminent engineer Joseph Mitchell, to survey the route. In a very old book, *The Scottish Tourist*, for which Sir Walter Scott wrote a commendation, the recom-

mended route to the south from Inverness, long before the days of railways, was exactly over the present track of the Highland main line, passing Daviot, Moy, the Slochd Mhuic pass and Carr Bridge. Mitchell's first proposal, strongly backed by such established authorities as Joseph Locke and his partner J. E. Errington, contained no more than a slight deviation from this, to pass through Nairn and then head almost directly south following the route of the present A939 highway to Ardclach and thence by the B9007. At that time, however, both were little more than bridle tracks. Thence the proposed line took the present route over the Pass of Druimuachdhar. Largely through his skill in ridicule, the leading counsel opposing the Bill secured its rejection on the grounds of the absurdity of attempting to take a railway over such mountain altitudes.

In the meantime the Invernessians had been carrying their railway along the shores of the Moray Firth, to block the rival project centred upon Aberdeen, which proposed a line to Inverness; and when the time was judged to be ripe for another attempt to get a line through to Perth it was Forres, and not Nairn, that was to be the northern springboard. This time they were successful, and the Inverness and Perth Junction Railway, as it was first known, opened for business in September 1863. While south of Aviemore the

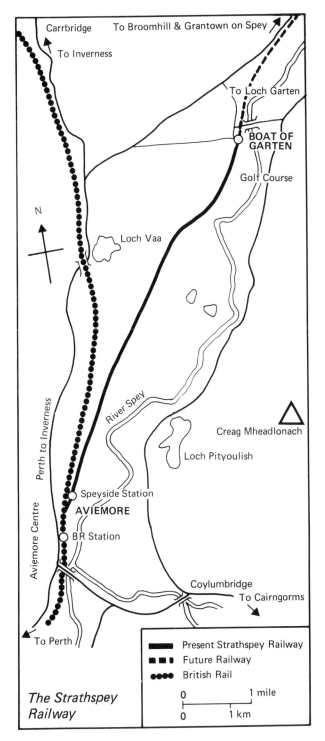

Carrbridge
To Broomhill & Grantown on Spey
To Inverness
To Loch Garten
BOAT OF GARTEN
Golf Course
N
Loch Vaa
River Spey
Creag Mheadlonach
Loch Pityoulish
Perth to Inverness
Speyside Station
AVIEMORE
BR Station
Aviemore Centre
Coylumbridge
To Cairngorms
To Perth
Present Strathspey Railway
Future Railway
British Rail
0   1 mile
0   1 km
The Strathspey Railway

route was as Mitchell originally intended, at the northern end legal battles and early opposition had resulted in a long detour. By the eagle's flight the distance from Aviemore to Inverness is only a little over twenty-five miles, but by the Highland Railway of 1863 it was just over sixty. Not anything of a race track either, because although in the neighbourhood of Aviemore it ran at river level grades, to reach Forres it had to cross the high and indescribably desolate watershed between the valleys of the Spey and the Findhorn, on gradients as severe as any in climbing to the Inverness-Perth County March in the Pass of Druimuachdhar.

Be that as it may, the line we now contemplate from a diesel-hauled British Railways express speeding down from Carr Bridge was for thirty-five years part of the main line from Inverness to Perth. Going north from Aviemore the first station was Boat of Garten, and there a most curious situation existed right up to the time when the railways were nationalized in 1948. The Highland Line was double-tracked through the station, and southbound trains were accommodated at a broad island platform, on the far side of which came trains of the Great North of Scotland Railway. This latter line was in constant conflict with the Highland in attempting to get an independent line of its own to Inverness. A line was enterprised from Craigellachie up Strathspey, but Parliamentary authorization extended no further than Broomhill, four and a quarter miles short of Boat of Garten. There a junction with the Highland main line was to be made. But in view of the 'cat and dog' relations that continued to exist between the two companies some diplomatist thought it would be better not to have them on the same tracks. Although the legal arrangements gave the Great North of Scotland running powers over the Highland line as far as Boat of Garten, the Highland laid down an entirely separate pair of rails alongside their own which made an end-on junction with the G N S R at Broomhill, and enabled the latter to run entirely on their own to the eastern side of the bay platform at Boat of Garten.

In due course amicable relations were estab-

111

Boat of Garten, before closing: looking towards Aviemore, with snow on the distant Cairngorm Mountains, in July! An ex-Great North of Scotland 4-4-0 is leaving with a train for Craigellachie

W. A. Camwell

lished, and useful connecting services were run between the two lines. It became more advantageous for passengers from stations on the Speyside line from Craigellachie to travel to Boat of Garten and then change into a Highland train for the south than to go the other way, entirely by the Great North of Scotland line to Aberdeen, and thence by one of the two main routes, either North British or Caledonian. In the early days of the Highland Railway all trains called at Boat of Garten, as they did at every other station on the line north of Blair Atholl; but Aviemore was not the important locomotive staging point that it afterwards became. In the ordinary way engines stationed at Perth did not work north of Kingussie, and the section from there northward through Boat of Garten was worked by Forres engines and men. It was the construction of the Inverness Direct Line, over precisely the road route indicated in *The Scottish Tourist*, and its opening in 1898, that wrought a complete metamorphosis in the trains working in this area, and was the first link in the long chain of circumstances leading to the formation of the present privately owned Strathspey Railway.

Very soon after the opening of the new direct line from Inverness to Aviemore and the arrival of the first of the 'Castle' class 4-6-0 locomotives, the rostering on the top link duties was changed so that on the majority of trains one engine worked through between Inverness and Perth. The big 4-6-0s were concentrated at each end, and Aviemore shed, like Forres, became concerned with providing pilots for heavy trains up to Slocdh, or to Dalnaspidal. Furthermore, many trains to and from the south henceforth carried sections serving both the old and the new line, and it became customary on some through-trains for the 4-6-0 engine to take the section for Grantown, Forres and Nairn, leaving one of the smaller Aviemore-based engines to take the lighter direct-line portion through to Inverness.

At one time Aviemore became a minor graveyard for locomotives awaiting scrapping or disposal. Space was always at a premium in the constrained area outside Lochgorm works at Inverness, and in the back siding at Aviemore, looking forlorn, forgotten and increasingly derelict, there were sometimes a few of the older Jones 4-4-0s that had been taken out of service. My recollection of them, however, is that they were in far better condition than many of the engines that have been rescued from the notorious Barry scrap yard in recent years! In the meantime Aviemore remained a busy centre from the locomotive point of view, but at the turn of the century and for some time afterwards it was not much concerned with passengers. It took its name from the Aviemore Inn which was used by some hardy nineteenth-century tourists as the starting point for a walk through the Larig Pass to Braemar. The station was sited a little to the north of the road junction between the direct track from Inverness and the one from Strathspey, where there was also a bridge over the river. At first it was no more than a wayside halting place in the earlier days of the Highland Railway, but all changed when the new direct line was built.

The provision of platforms, track facilities and sidings then became most lavish, and on the down platform was the skilfully sheltered covered area. Junction stations in Great Britain are reputedly not health resorts, and however long the platform awnings may be, wind, driving rain or snow can whistle through with merciless abandon — as anyone like myself who had frequent experience of changing trains at Carnforth or Hellifield will testify! In the new Aviemore, however, the ends of the covered area were closed in, with handsomely designed, fully glazed walls. I often wondered why, because when I first knew the station some sixty years ago the passenger interchange activity was minimal. The halcyon days of Aviemore as a winter sports centre had not even been glimpsed on the far horizon. There was more activity on the less sheltered up island platform, when Forres and direct-line sections of trains for the south arrived simultaneously and much remarshalling of through carriages took place.

The pilot engine working from the engine shed that now forms the locomotive base of the Strathspey Steam Railway was interesting, and sometimes peculiar. The introduction of David Jones's very splendid 'Loch' class 4-4-0s in 1896 brought about the transition from the old method of working the line, section by section, because it was found that by provision of pilots at strategic points these capable 4-4-0 engines could work the trains through between Inverness and Perth. The way it was done may seem a bit odd today. On the principal afternoon train to the south, for example, one of the older, highly distinctive Jones 4-4-0s of the 'Duke' or 'F' class would couple on ahead of the train engine at Forres to help in the long 1 in 70 pull up to Dava summit. Thence the pilot would continue at the head of the train during the downhill run into Strathspey, through Boat of Garten and Aviemore — the latter still in its 'wayside' days — to Kingussie. There the pilot would transfer from front to rear of the train to provide rear-end banking up to Druimuachdhar summit, then known as County March loop.

When I first knew Aviemore, not long after World War I, the pilots and local train engines were the Drummond 'Small Ben' class 4-4-0s, and one or two 'Lochs' that had been rebuilt with larger Caledonian type boilers. But they had one of the larger-boilered 'Bens' during the summer months, for a time *Ben-na-Caillich*, for the direct-line section of the noon tourist express from Perth. The train engine working through to Inverness took the Forres line section of the train. Visiting Aviemore in early March 1938, and making my way down from the station to the engine shed, the 'lost legion' on the siding outside had disappeared, but inside, in completely original condition, was a Drummond 'Barney' 0-6-0. By that time nearly all the smaller Drummond engines on the Highland had had the distinctive safety valves on the top of their domes removed to a position over the firebox. In the case of the 'Barneys' this made them almost indistinguishable from their McIntosh counterparts on the Caledonian. But this Barney was in pristine condition, fitted significantly with one of the big ploughs used for charging snowdrifts. Aviemore was the nearest locomotive shed to the dreaded Dava Moor, scene of some of the worst snow-blocks in Highland railway history.

The coming of the Stanier 'Black Five' 4-6-0s in 1934—5, of which No. 5025 on the Strathspey line of today is so rightly-cherished an example, altered the whole character of the engine working at Aviemore. Then, for the first time in its history, the Highland became possessed of a superfluity of engines — very large and powerful ones, too. I became conscious of this in particular one snowy winter's night at Aviemore in 1935. I had an engine pass for the day, and had ridden north in the early morning of the same day on the engines of the Mail. When it came to returning in the evening I was prepared to travel to Perth either by the up Mail or by the London 'sleeper'. The former was not unduly heavy, but a second 'Black Five', working home, was coupled on ahead as pilot. I let this train go and, muffled up in my overalls, waited for the London train. It came in with a single 'Black Five', but just as I was about to present my credentials to the driver and climb up, another 'Black Five' came backing down out of the darkness to couple on. I sought the comfort of the train itself on that snowy night!

When the minions of the 'good Doctor' came north and decided that alternative routes from Aviemore to Inverness were too much of a luxury, I often wondered if the engineering departments were not secretly glad to be rid of the line down to Forres. Sociologically, the severing of the direct line from Forres through Grantown-on-Spey to the south was a disaster. One could still get from Forres to the south via Elgin and Huntly but Grantown, that most gracious of Highland towns, was completely isolated. Engineering-wise the line over Dava Moor was a perennial headache. Like the line at the Fairy Hillocks, the dreaded Sutherland-Caithness County March, the menace was the completely exposed nature of the line over the moorland, and even with modern equipment they could not immediately clear the effects of severe drifting during the winter of 1962–3.

Two years later news was given in the *Railway Magazine* of ministerial consent to the withdrawal of all passenger services between Aviemore and Forres, which of course was no more than the first step towards the closing of the line itself. In the years just before that fatal March when I was doing the fieldwork for my book on the Highland Railway, the air was thick with threats of the closure of the whole railway system north and west of Inverness; but while I was able to insert, at final proof stage, a reference to the relief felt that the Minister had refused his consent to this altogether brutal proposal, there was hardly a word about the Aviemore-Forres line. In fact, I have had to search through the small print of the *Railway Magazine* of the mid-1960s to find any reference to it at all. My own professional and literary work was then taking me to far different fields, and no devoted Scot arose to write a scholarly obituary of the Aviemore-Forres line, or to enter a plea of any kind for its preservation. Yet apart from its rather grisly claim to notoriety on Dava Moor it included one of the finest architectural works on the whole of the Highland Railway, in the seven-arch viaduct over the Divie, ten miles south of Forres. It was 477 ft long and 106 ft from the river bed to the top of the parapet — very graceful and containing some fine ornamental stone work.

That any part of the line was preserved was due not to former Highland Railway interests, strong though they were, but to the interposition of traffic from the one-time Great North of Scotland line at Boat of Garten. Until 4 November 1968 a daily pick-up goods train, diesel-hauled of course, left Aviemore, not for Forres, but for Craigellachie, and returned at 14.00 hours, mainly for malt distillery traffic. The speeds were not meteoric, but the track was kept in presentable condition by the occasional running of a weed-killing special. But it was to close in November 1968 and it would have done, but for the determination and sustained hard work of the Strathspey Railway Association. Its aim was ultimately to re-open the line between Aviemore and Grantown-on-Spey, but very wisely all efforts were concentrated on a modest

Boat of Garten, in 1977, with saddle-tank No. 9, Hunslet 'Austerity' 0-6-0 in foreground   *Brian Morrison*

beginning where the rails were still *in situ*, as far as Boat of Garten. By excellent public relations work the interest of the Highland and Islands Development Board was secured, and assistance in labour was obtained from a Manpower Services Commission's Job Creation team. Members of the Strathspey Railway Association showed that they meant business, and that they were capable of doing it in no half-hearted or amateurish way.

Their restoration of the station at Boat of Garten received a Civic Trust award for its excellence, and their enterprise in obtaining other items of true Highland Railway lineage is shown in the purchase

of items from stations on other parts of the line, the sites of which were doomed to obliteration under the Beeching closures. Fine examples are the handsome iron footbridge from Dalnaspidal, which has been re-erected at Boat of Garten to replace an identical one removed in 1960, and station building material which is to be used in the new Speyside station at Aviemore. Perhaps the most remarkable example of the esteem in which the Strathspey Railway has established itself locally has been at Grantown-on-Spey. Since the line was closed in 1965 the station buildings there have been boarded up, and the wide canopy over the platform and the large glass screens at each end have fallen into disrepair. And when the Highland Regional Council announced its intention of purchasing and developing the site it was feared that nothing short of demolition and total clearance would ensue. Nothing has proved to be further from the case.

The preserved Caledonian 0-6-0—repainted in its beautiful pre-grouping colours—which has now been sent to Aviemore for service on the Strathspey Railway   *Courtesy: Ind Coope Alloa Brewery Co Ltd*

The Highland Regional Council evidently appreciate that a preserved steam railway to their most gracious burgh would be an immense tourist attraction, and 'development' work in the station area will include preservation of all the buildings and ensuring that no enroachment on the space required for sidings and so on takes place. The nearest rails are at present seven and a half miles away. This is not far in ordinary railway statistical considerations, but to an organization largely dependent on volunteer labour it is a very long way! Nevertheless the Council seems happy to keep things intact at Grantown pending the arrival of the rails and the trains.

In the meantime locomotives and rolling stock have been accumulating at Aviemore. The old Highland running shed was a commodious one of four roads and this is being re-equipped to provide for repair and maintenance of locomotives. The new turntable is that on which so many Highland locomotives posed for their photographs at Kyle of Lochalsh, while the water-column, also of vintage Highland design, comes from Forsinard, up near the Sutherland-Caithness County March. It became known to the men-of-the-fleet who endured long-drawn-out journeys to the ships based at Scapa Flow as 'Frozen-hard', referring, one hopes, to the state of the ground and not to the contents of the water column!

The 'flagship' of the Strathspey Railway locomotive fleet is of course the Stanier 'Black Five' 4-6-0 — with all due respect to that most distinguished recent addition, the Caledonian 0-6-0 No. 828, owned by the Scottish Locomotive Preservation Trust, and hitherto ensconced in the Glasgow Transport Museum. But the 'Black Five' No. 5025 is rather a 'special' so far as the Highland is concerned. She is one of the very first engines of that numerous class, and only the sixth to be delivered. In 1934 orders were placed for no fewer than seventy engines of this new type, twenty from Crewe works and fifty from the Vulcan Foundry. Although the running numbers 5000 — 5019 were allocated to the Crewe batch the Vulcans were first out, and engine No. 5020 posed for the photograph from which the railway world at large learned what this subsequently very familiar class looked like. The first ten from Vulcans were all earmarked for the Highland, though No. 5020 was for a time retained in England for dynamometer car trials and other experimental work. The Speyside Railway is honoured in having an engine of the very first batch of this famous class, older by several months than the 'class leader' No. 5000 owned by the National Railway Museum at York. Moreover, unlike the majority of the other preserved members of the class, No. 5025 retains the original form of domeless boiler. Its preservation was due to Mr W. E. C. Watkinson.

A word in conclusion about names: strangers to Strathspey may wonder at the origin or significance of 'Boat of Garten'. There are several places in the north-eastern parts of the Highlands with the prefix 'boat'. They perpetuate the site of old ferries, and others that may be mentioned are Boat of Don, and strangely Boat O' Bridge, further down the Spey. Garten itself is an anglicized version of the Gaelic word *gairtean* which means a field of corn. It marks the northern end of the great forest of Rothiemurchus which covered a vast area in Strathspey, from Kingussie northward. Boat of Garten meant the ferry by the cornfield.

THE SEVERN VALLEY RAILWAY

Some people imagine that because of my lifelong pursuit of railwayana in all its vast diversity I am familiar with every nook and cranny into which the iron road has penetrated, and they are very surprised to learn there are places where I have not yet been. There are, of course, bound to be some dark areas, and until a short time ago, one of these was the stretch of the River Severn between Worcester and Shrewsbury. This might seem all the more surprising in that my family connections in the north-west corner of Worcestershire extend back for many, many generations; but my own parents moved south when I was no more than a few months old, and of personal associations I had none, until a few months ago.

Furthermore, the line following the Severn Valley upstream through Bewdley and Bridgnorth must have been one of the least documented and less publicized of all branch lines. In MacDermot's classic history of the Great Western Railway it is dismissed in a single sentence. It had not the remotest pretensions to being a trunk line. No great express detached through carriages to run its length, and so far as motive power was concerned it could well have been called the Lazarus of the West Midland area. How then did it rise to such heights that its present owners could claim it as 'Britain's leading steam railway'? The Severn Valley began as an entirely independent concern.

It was no protégé or offshoot of the Oxford, Worcester and Wolverhampton, and it had its own very beautiful heraldic device. The Romans' name for the River Severn was Sabrina, and on the seal the lady is shown in contemplative mood among the reeds on its banks.

There were no half measures about the beginnings of the Severn Valley Railway. The promoters brought in some of the most eminent men of the day; the fact that Thomas Brassey was the principal contractor was a guarantee that the work would be superbly done. One has only to look at some of the masonry to be sure of this. The original line ran from a junction with the Shrewsbury and Hereford Railway at Sutton Bridge, about one and a half miles south of Shrewsbury itself, and ran through Buildwas, Coalport, Bridgnorth and Bewdley to a junction with the O W & W at Hartlebury, a distance of forty and three-quarter miles. The line for the most part followed what the Americans would call 'river level grades', and south of Bridgnorth it passed through some of the most beautiful scenery in the entire course of the River Severn. From the very outset, the line passed beside the very symbol of the Industrial Revolution in England, 'Ironbridge', a magnificent work of which the bicentenary was happily and fittingly celebrated two years ago. This incredibly beautiful com-

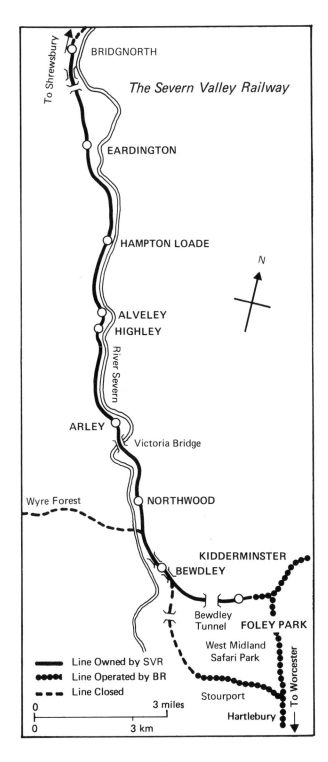

The Severn Valley Railway

To Shrewsbury
BRIDGNORTH
EARDINGTON
HAMPTON LOADE

N

ALVELEY
HIGHLEY

River Severn

ARLEY
Victoria Bridge

Wyre Forest
NORTHWOOD

KIDDERMINSTER
BEWDLEY

Bewdley
Tunnel   FOLEY PARK

West Midland
Safari Park

To Worcester

Stourport

Hartlebury

Line Owned by SVR
Line Operated by BR
Line Closed

0   3 miles
0   3 km

bination of architecture and engineering brought visitors from all over the world. However, by the time the Severn Valley Railway Company was incorporated, in 1853, there were greater and more recent constructional wonders to be seen in England, and the appeal of Ironbridge became somewhat diminished.

Furthermore, the use of cast iron as a bridge material had been thrown into considerable disrepute, both in the popular and technical mind, by the serious accident on the Dee viaduct just outside Chester in May 1847. This viaduct had been designed by Robert Stephenson as part of the works of the Chester and Holyhead Railway, but the Shrewsbury and Chester Railway had running powers over this line as far as Saltney Junction, and it was one of the latter company's trains that suffered when one of the cast iron girders broke, and the whole train except for the engine and tender fell into the river. No one except the driver escaped; five persons were killed, and all the remaining thirty-one on board injured, some seriously. The disaster did nothing to enhance the reputation of Robert Stephenson, because the Inspecting Officer carrying out the inquiry on behalf of the Board of Trade severely criticized the design of the bridge girders. Yet cast iron in itself, when properly applied, is an eminently suitable material for arched bridges, though one can appreciate that those responsible were not over-anxious to publicize the completion in the Severn Valley of two cast iron arched bridges of twice the span of the famous pioneer work at Ironbridge.

The engineering world learned of John Fowler's magnificent creations at Arley and near Buildwas in quite an indirect way. At the Institution of Civil Engineers, during its 1867-8 session, papers were presented on the construction of the large bridge over the River Thames built by the Victoria Station and Pimlico Railway to give access to a new terminal station on the north bank of the river. In the discussion on these papers, almost incidentally, a certain J. D. Baldry, in wondering why the authors had used wrought iron rather than cast iron in the bridge over the Thames, thought 'it

119

might be interesting to place on record the particulars of a cast iron bridge, of a larger span than the bridge under consideration; and by permission of Mr John Fowler, Past President, Inst.C.E., would do so. There were two bridges of this description — one on the Severn Valley Railway, the other on the Coalbrookdale Railway, and both were erected over the River Severn.' The former, which had been brought in service in 1862 was, of course, the much cherished Victoria Bridge at Arley, the civil engineering 'lion' of the Severn Valley Railway of today. Its twin was not on the railway itself but on the line from Wellington, which crossed the Severn just before intersecting the now-abandoned part of the S V R at Buildwas.

In that discussion, as subsequently reported in the proceedings of the Institution, Mr Baldry was not sparing in the details that he gave about the bridge; neither did the Institution itself refrain from publishing a magnificent set of working drawings. The bridge was designed for a double line of railway, and there were four arches, each positioned immediately below one of the running rails. These four main arches were each cast in nine parts. Great care was taken in fitting the cast cross-bracing frames, and in all the bolted connections the bolts were tightly fitted into their respective holes, and the joints keyed up closely. In reading of the technical excellence of the workmanship put into the job one thinks rather sadly of the terrible contrast this made to the constructional details of the first Tay Bridge, and the shoddy workmanship which, almost as much as its bad design, was the cause of its disastrous end. But never forget, at the Victoria Bridge near Arley Thomas Brassey was the responsible contractor. Its designer, John Fowler, was subsequently the designer of the Forth Bridge. Many years before he designed the cast iron arched bridges in the Severn Valley Fowler had been to see

The magnificent cast iron viaduct over the River Severn near Arley, with ex-L M S 0-6-0T hauling a train for Bridgnorth, April 1978   *John Titlow*

120

Victoria Bridge: a close-up showing fine detail of the arch

Severn Valley Railway

Brunel's famous bridge at Maidenhead when there had been some alarm over a subsidence, and some cracking. He thought it was in a dangerous condition, but added that '...the centring is a very excellent and scientific one, the whole of the timbers being in a state of thrust'. It may well have been the design of Brunel's centring for the Maidenhead arches that encouraged him to such a spectacular design in the Severn Valley, using cast iron 'in a state of thrust'.

The celebrated Royal Engineer Officer Captain H. W. Tyler carried out the inspection on behalf of the Board of Trade, and he contributed to the discussion at the Institution of Civil Engineers. He said:

... it had been his duty to inspect and test the bridge over the River Severn which had just been described, and he was happy to bear testimony to its excellence. It was, in his opinion, a great improvement upon the Victoria Bridge previously constructed over the River Thames. It combined stiffness with cheapness to a remarkable degree, and he had been, for that reason, much struck with it. He thought there was an advantage in the employment of cast iron, in the place of wrought iron, in bridges of this description. In the first place, wrought iron was less durable, and required more painting; in the second place, cast iron bridges, even of large spans, could be constructed with greater cheapness; and in the third place, cast iron was the material best adapted to resist compression.

He then went on to make some comparisons, between the bridge and the one over the Thames, not altogether favourable to the latter!

A later speaker in the discussion referred to the amazingly low cost of the bridge, namely a little over £11,000. He went on to say:

In consequence of being obliged to make a separate pattern for every segment of the rib of the arch, he did not think a cast iron bridge could be made with such expedition as a bridge of wrought iron, although he agreed that cast iron was the proper material for an arch; and probably that circumstance might have influenced Mr Fowler in using wrought iron for the Victoria Bridge, which had to be finished within a limited time. The latter was erected in a little over twelve months, whereas the bridge of the River Severn was nearly two years in construction. It might have been completed in less time, but there was always a much greater amount of fitting and variety of parts in cast iron structures.

The Severn Valley Railway remained an independent company until 1870 when it was absorbed into the Great Western. From the outset it was operated by the West Midland Railway, of which the somewhat notorious Oxford, Worcester and Wolverhampton — 'Old Worse and Worse' — was the constituent immediately responsible. It was never more than one of the byways of the British railway network, though prior to the opening of the short route to Birmingham and the North, via Bicester, the distance from Paddington to Shrewsbury, via the Severn Valley line, was only one mile longer than via Birmingham and Wolverhampton, 172½ against 171½ miles. There is no record, however, or even a suggestion that a through express service might be worked up that way. Nevertheless, PADDINGTON, WORCESTER, BEWDLEY, BRIDGNORTH & SHREWSBURY would have looked imposing on the carriage roof boards! In the last years before World War II there were five through trains daily between Worcester and Shrewsbury: the quickest took two hours nineteen minutes for the journey of fifty-two miles, stopping at all intermediate stations, but most of the trains took considerably longer.

Train for Bridgnorth leaving Arley hauled by British Railways standard 2-6-4T No. 80079, March 1978
Severn Valley Railway

After the war, traffic on the line jogged along in the same old way, no better and no worse than many another branch line; but nothing could save it from the effects of the Beeching 'blitz'. The surprising thing was that when proposals were launched for preserving and operating part of the line there should have been so much *local* opposition. In other parts of this book I have told of how local residents rose in wrath against ministerial proposals for closure; but in the Severn Valley, the Shropshire County Council, the Chelmarsh Parish Council, and certain intransigent and ill-informed individuals formed a united front to try and prevent the granting of a Light Railway Order to enable the line south of Bridgnorth to be operated after it had been purchased from British Railways. All that, happily, is now past history, and since the re-opening of the first part of the line in 1970, the Severn Valley Railway has gone from strength to strength, to become in many ways one of the most remarkable of all the privately owned railways in Britain.

Examining its 'vital statistics' it becomes evident that its locomotive stock includes a far higher proportion of main line to industrial units than any of the others. The previous ownership is predominantly Great Western, and a sustained attempt has been made to retain the Great Western character of the line. But while the basic passenger operation is over the twelve and a half miles between Bewdley and Bridgnorth, the southward continuation over one arm of the Bewdley-Kidderminster-Hartlebury triangle has been kept open, and it is available for the acceptance from British Railways of excursions from any part of the country. Its own trains, in the height of the summer season, must be the heaviest regularly run on any private steam railway, because they are made up to ten coaches, the maximum that can be accommodated at the platforms at Bridgnorth and Bewdley. An attempt is made to keep the rakes as

Train from Bridgnorth arriving at Bewdley, hauled by ex-G W R 2-6-2T No. 4566   *Severn Valley Railway*

of all-G W R, or all-L M S formation and arrange for their haulage by appropriate locomotives. Although the latest tally published was of fourteen Great Western locomotives, against eleven L M S, or L M S orientated 'standards', by no means all of these would be capable of handling maximum load trains without assistance.

In its rejuvenation the Severn Valley has cast off any suspicions that it might be merely a by-way. The large main line engines regularly working over it include Great Western 'Halls', '51XX' class 2-6-2 tanks, and at least one '28XX' 2-8-0 freighter. The L M S representatives include 'Black Five' 4-6-0s, an '8F' Stanier 2-8-0, and one of the Stanier 2-6-0s — his first main line type for the L M S, the first of which caused something of a sensation at Crewe. The preserved engine on the Severn Valley Railway, like the pioneer engine of the class, has a domeless boiler, and it first emerged from Crewe Works with a safety-valve bonnet of unmistakably Great Western style supporting the top feed clack valves. Apparently someone in high authority on the L M S thought this was betraying the Great Western influence a little too obviously, and ordered it off, but not before the ever watchful W. H. Whitworth had photographed it!

The ex-G W R large 2-6-2T No. 5164 newly outshopped from Bridgnorth and in magnificent condition at Bewdley, November 1980   *O. S. Nock*

The ex-L M S Stanier 2-6-0 No. 42968 at Bridgnorth for repairs
D. J. Montgomery

The fact that an engine with a maximum axle load of 20.15 tons, heavier than any of the loadings on the G W and L M S 4-6-0s, could be accepted, was indeed a tribute to the design and construction of the Victoria Bridge at Arley, because while it is true that it was designed for double-line traffic, such axle loadings can hardly have been contemplated at the time. The Stanier 2-6-0 from the L M S has, indeed, an adhesion weight of no less than 59.5 tons, 3.5 tons greater than that of the Horwich 'crab', which it succeeded. The largest

and heaviest engine ever to run on the line was the B R class 7 standard 4-6-2 *Britannia* with an overall length of 68 ft 9 in., and an all-up weight of 143.15 tons. Her maximum axle load was only slightly greater than that of the Stanier 2-6-0, 20.25 tons; but a concentration of 60.75 tons over a wheelbase of no more than 14 ft, compared to the 59.5 tons over 16 ft 6in. on the 2-6-0, represented a far greater centralized mass, and *Britannia*, as reported elsewhere in this book, has now departed for the Nene Valley Railway. So far as length and total weight is concerned *Britannia* was only slightly greater than the magnificent Longmoor 2-10-0 *Gordon*, 67 ft 6¼ in. overall, and weighing 133.8 tons. But *Gordon* has ten coupled wheels, and his maximum axle load is only 13.45 tons.

When my friends of the Severn Valley Railway invited me to see some of their winter activities I recalled my only previous associations with the district, neither of which, as it happened, involved personal visits. In my last year as an undergraduate at Imperial College, a brief vacational visit at Easter was arranged in order to do some river-flow gauging on the Severn at Bewdley. As it turned out I had no sooner arrived home at Barrow from the spring term when it was discovered that I had a mild attack of scarlet fever, and instead of going to Bewdley I spent the entire vacation in quarantine! The other association came in the 1930s, when among all my other duties at Westinghouse I was mechanical engineer responsible for design of pneumatic equipment for collieries. The marketing for this modest increment to our business was done mostly on a personal basis by an agent resident in Sheffield. He was a bluff old Yorkshireman, who seemed to have connections with every colliery manager in the West Riding, so it was a surprise to us in London when he landed a small order from the Highley Mining Company, at their Alveley Colliery. I must admit we had to get an atlas to find out where it was, and even then we were not much wiser! Coal from this area had formed a not-inconsiderable volume of traffic in the earlier days of the Severn Valley Railway. The job at Alveley Colliery was a straightforward one, and involved nought but standard equipment. So there was no occasion for me to pay a visit, and it was not until the autumn of 1980 that I first saw the beautiful old town of Bewdley.

One's immediate impression of the station is of the true Great Western atmosphere, accentuated of course by the profusion of lower quadrant signals, but it is at the Bridgnorth end that the true magnitude of the whole operation becomes evident. The rails stop short just to the north of the

The ex-War Department 2-10-0, at one time attached to the Longmoor Military Railway, No. 600 *Gordon* at Highley with an enthusiasts' special from Bridgnorth to Bewdley, April 1977   *David Eatwell*

station, beyond which the original line tunnelled under the town to continue towards Shrewsbury; but in that relatively short space a veritable locomotive 'main works' has been created! The old Great Western goods shed provided the enveloping fabric for this enterprise, and within it have already been gathered and put to good and expert use heavy machinery from many of the 'steam' works now converted to more modern forms of power. Furthermore the management of the Severn Valley Railway has, through the skill and devotion of its staff, established an enviable reputation for reliable work, so much so that now they carry out heavy repairs not only on their own locomotives, but undertake it for other private railways as well.

When I had the pleasure of visiting Bridgnorth I saw no fewer than *three* celebrated visitors in varying states of 'undress', if I may call it so. There was the celebrated Stanier 'Jubilee' class three-cylinder 4-6-0 No. 5690 *Leander*, which in recent years has done such yeoman work in hauling the British Railways steam specials from Carnforth, and which cut such a splendid figure in the 'Rocket-150' parade at Rainhill in May 1980. There is much more to be said about this engine in the chapter dealing with the excursions from Carnforth. Another celebrated engine undergoing a 'heavy general' at Bridgnorth was the Gresley 'K4' 2-6-0 No. 3442 *The Great Marquess*, owned by Lord Garnock. I have the most vivid recollections of the first introduction of these very powerful engines on the West Highland line in 1937, and of riding on the first of them. It was originally painted black and named *Loch Long*, but I was glad to see that the batch of five that followed in 1938 were finished in apple green and named after clan chieftains of the West Highlands. Those initially responsible for the choice of those names got rather mixed up when they ventured into the

Train from B R line at Kidderminster, near Bewdley, hauled by ex-G W R 4-6-0 No. 7812 *Erlestoke Manor*
Steve le Cheminant

Ready for the day's work at Bridgnorth, left to right:
L M S 4-6-0 *Leander*; G W R 4-6-0 *Hinton Manor*;
L M S Ivatt 2-6-0 No. 43106; behind the latter, G W R
0-6-0 No. 3205   *Severn Valley Railway*

Gaelic over some of them. *The Great Marquess* was a notable exception but on seeing that beautiful engine I am always reminded of some stirring footplate runs I made on two other members of the class, between Fort William and Crianlarich, in wild and typical West Highland weather.

Most intriguing of all among engines in the works at Bridgnorth was none other than the L N W R 8 ft 6 in. 2-2-2 *Cornwall*. It was, of course, hoped that she might be able to run in the Rocket-150 parade in May 1980, but the preliminary examinations, long previous to the event, revealed that her boiler was in no state to be steamed. So she has come to Bridgnorth to await attention and in all probability an entirely new boiler. At one time the idea of such a renovation would have been summarily dismissed as just 'not on'; but in these far happier days of railway preservation it would be unthinkable to have such a relic and not run her! With the news that a working replica of Richard Trevithick's Pen-y-Darran engine is being constructed, could we not look forward to an actual staging of the juxtaposition, so vividly painted by Terence Cuneo, of *Pen-y-Darran* and *Cornwall*, as representing the work of the Trevithicks, father and son.

The celebrated L N W R 8 ft 6 in. 2-2-2 *Cornwall* in Bridgnorth works for repairs, September 1979

Ken Bull

134

Ex-L M S 2-6-0 No. 6443 at Bridgnorth station
Charles P. Friel

While a majority of the visitors who come annually to the Severn Valley Railway in their thousands do so to enjoy the train ride hauled by steam, and many record by both camera and sound the railway features of the journey, the line is equally fortunate in the exquisite beauty of the country through which it runs. As a traveller who has seen a good deal of the world in both hemispheres, I would say that there is nothing on earth to compare with the river scenery of England, and I cannot imagine a more lovely example than the Severn near Arley. In the next chapter I refer to the Furness Railway swooping upon A. Heaton Cooper's paintings of the Lake District for advertising purposes some seventy years ago. In the sumptuously illustrated series of books published by A. & C. Black there was one, with paintings by Sutton Palmer, on the *Rivers and Streams of England*, and if the Severn Valley Railway should ever light upon the illustration depicting the river near Arley I am sure they would snatch it up for it is exquisite, no other word for it!

13

Lakeside And Haverthwaite

I have always had a great affection for the branch of the Furness Railway to Windermere Lakeside, though oddly enough my first acquaintance with it was made with some boyish reluctance. The year was 1916, and we had not long moved into the house the bank had bought for my father's occupation in Barrow. It was on an estate ringed by a belt of trees, and while most of the long narrow strip of garden consisted of formal flower beds and trim lawns, it led into what we called 'the wood', where the previous owner had built a beautiful fernery. There I had begun to scheme out the track layout for a model railway, and I was thus engaged one Saturday afternoon just after lunch, when my sister came running down the garden and said: 'Daddy's going to Windermere'. I was a bit tetchy at being disturbed. As it was so soon after moving in, my mother was absorbed with domestic matters and didn't come, so it was only the three of us who walked down to Furness Abbey station and took the 2.00 p.m. stopping train to Ulverston. There the branch local for Lakeside was waiting in a siding to the north of the station, and after a wait of no more than seven minutes we were off again, hauled by one of the smart Pettigrew 4-4-2 tank engines. The first two of these engines had been newly introduced in 1914.

By that time my tetchiness had completely vanished. From my earliest school days geography had always been a favourite subject and as we turned from the Furness main line at Plumpton Junction, and the beautiful estuarine scenery of the River Leven opened out on the right-hand side of the line, I was entranced. It was double track at first, though my father pointed out the track of the curve that had at one time provided a direct connection from the eastern end of the Furness line. During the war the track had been lifted, and, so we were told, allocated to the ROD for use in France. The line beside the Leven estuary was double tracked as far as Greenodd, where there was one of those substantial stone-built station houses so characteristic of the Furness Railway. In later years I always felt that the line should have forked at Greenodd, with one line continuing straight on past Penny Bridge and Lowick Bridge to the foot of Coniston Water, which was only three and a half miles away. It would have seemed an easier way of getting to Coniston than through Broughton-in-Furness, and toiling uphill through Torver.

The Windermere Lakeside line swung round through almost a complete right angle to the right after leaving Greenodd, and an incident I saw a few years after the end of the war always makes me think, a little wistfully, about the role the present-day Lakeside and Haverthwaite Railway might have played if British Railways had not been so precipitate in lifting the rails from the triangle

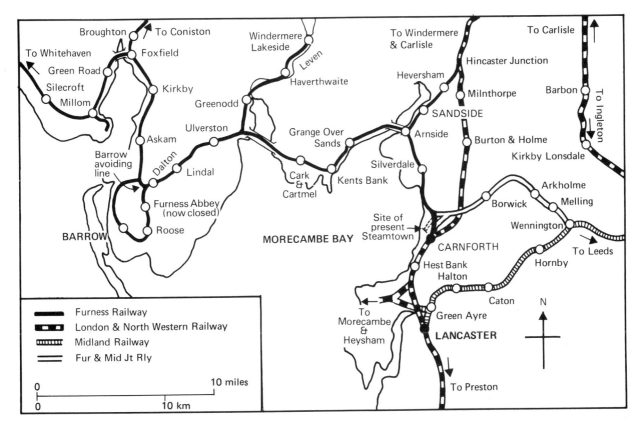

Furness Railway
London & North Western Railway
Midland Railway
Fur & Mid Jt Rly

junction at Plumpton. I was cycling back from Newby Bridge one day when I saw a complete train of Midland clerestory-roofed stock hauled by a Midland engine approaching Greenodd from the south; it slowed down to walking pace, to collect the tablet for the single-line section ahead, and then, gently gathering speed, it wound its way round the viaduct over the Crake River and headed towards Haverthwaite. It was a through excursion to Lakeside from the West Riding headed by a resplendent class '2' superheater 4-4-0. The direct link to the east at Plumpton had been reinstated by that time. What a splendid connecting link it would make today for steam-hauled excursions to Lakeside.

Talking of locomotives, the Pettigrew 4-4-2 tanks had only just taken over from the little 2-4-2s, which in their turn had been rebuilt from 2-4-0 mainline passenger engines dating from

1872. They were very pretty little things, yet becoming somewhat overpowered by increasing loads. When we first travelled to Lakeside there were six passenger trains daily in each direction, so scheduled that one tank engine could work the entire day's service. There could not have been much traffic in the quieter months of the year, and in 1905 Pettigrew built a steam rail motor car to deal with all the passenger business on the branch. This seated no more than twelve first class and thirty-six third class passengers. I never saw it in service as I travelled on the branch when there were many more people about. There were some quite stiff gradients to be negotiated. The line descended at 1 in 82-76-94 from Ulverston towards Plumpton Junction, which of course had to be climbed by inward bound trains from the branch, and 1 in 78-64-82-117 through Haverthwaite when heading towards Lakeside.

137

The gorge of the Leven, into which the railway climbed at Haverthwaite, was Wordsworth's favourite approach to the Lakes, and when I first knew it, it was a great deal more peaceful than it is today. Even then, however, the factory had come to Haverthwaite, likewise the forge and the Reckitt's 'blue' works to Backbarrow. It is sufficient commentary upon the infrequency of road traffic that the narrow highway—the *only* road from Barrow to the south!—took a hazardous S bend to drive clean through the middle of the 'blue' works. There is now a dual carriageway by-passing this very slight industrial area. W. T. Palmer, that most attractive writer of *Things seen on the English Lakes*, mildly deplored the presence of 'a roaring railroad' in the Leven gorge, but added: 'Oh! it's fine to be here when the first golden shaft of sunshine bends over the hills and the birds awake into active life.' At that hour, too, the folks in the little engine shed at Lakeside would be kindling the fire in the tank engine that was to work the first train of the day, the 8.40 a.m. This connected with the morning service from Barrow, which conveyed a through carriage to Euston.

I have before me the time-table for the winter service of 1906, and there was some extraordinarily close dovetailing of services at Ulverston, thus:

8.59 : 8.35 a.m. Grange to Barrow arrived
9.5 : 8.40 a.m. From Lakeside arrived
9.7 : 8.35 a.m. Grange to Barrow departed
9.13 : 6.40 a.m. Whitehaven-Carnforth/Euston arrived
9.15 : Local to Lakeside departed
9.17 : Carnforth (Euston) train departed

How all this was managed, with only two platform roads, I have no idea.

Reverting to our own first journey I recall how well my father had done his topographical homework on the route before we made that journey together and how, when we had passed the factories at Backbarrow, he drew my sister and me over to the right-hand side of the carriage to see 'a very pretty bridge'. This of course was Newby Bridge, not only an architectural gem in itself, but

set in almost sylvan scenery. Many years later I painted it in water colours from a photograph I took from the forecourt of the Swan Hotel, but the masterpiece came from A. Heaton Cooper, the man above all others who captured the spirit of the Lakeland scene. His viewpoint was from one of the windows of the hotel, and the Furness Railway liked it so much that they included it in full colour in their series of official picture postcards.

While Newby Bridge was no more than a single platform on the railway, devoid of any signals or points and described in the time-table as a 'motor platform' at which all trains made no more than conditional stops, it was a major road junction in Lakeland motoring and a favourite staging point in my own teenage cycling in the area. I am sorry to say that very few Barrovians of those days used the railway to get to the lakes. We had to leave home about twenty minutes before train departure times at Furness Abbey station, and that afternoon train leaving at 2.00 p.m., through the connection at Ulverston, reached Newby Bridge at 2.45 p.m. and Lakeside at 2.50 p.m., a journey time of sixty-five minutes, which I did regularly in seventy-two to seventy-five minutes on a push bike. We thought little of that delightful period piece of a railway that ran from Ulverston to Lakeside. My own thoughts were directed further east to the London and North Western main line over Shap. When we travelled on the Lakeside line our trains were frequently held up for up to ten minutes at Haverthwaite to cross another coming in the opposite direction, which led my father to suggest that the station name should be changed to 'Have-a-wait'. He was so pleased with this little jest that he once tried it on A. R. Aslett, the General Manager, at a business gathering in Barrow. From all accounts the 'GM' was not amused! From a study of the time-table of the day it would appear that the opposing trains for which we had to wait were either goods or excursions.

At the time of grouping the Furness section came into the Western 'B' Division, of which by far the largest constituent was the former Lancashire and Yorkshire Railway. When visiting the works at Barrow I remember Edward Sharples, the mechanical engineer of the line, showing me the new engine diagram book, including of course the big Horwich four-cylinder 4-6-0s recently rebuilt and superheated. In the circumstances of grouping, and with the need to reduce as quickly as possible the number of different designs of locomotives, the Furness engines did not last long, and within a short time workings on the Lakeside branch had been taken over by Aspinall 2-4-2 tanks of the standard Lancashire and Yorkshire design, equipped for push-and-pull working to eliminate light engine movements at Ulverston and Lakeside. By the end of World War II even these had gone, and when I travelled from Ambleside to Barrow in 1946, the train waiting for us at Lakeside was headed by a Stanier class '3' 2-6-2 tank.

There was much optimism about an impending revival of trade in the mid-1950s, and in its issue of 22 June 1957 *Modern Transport* carried an article entitled 'Where business is booming', dealing with the railway and transport problems in Furness and West Cumberland. Particular mention was made in this article of the Reckitt's 'blue' industry at Backbarrow, and of a small specialist steel plant in the same village that produced alloys for surgical instruments. Hope doomed to die, as far as the railway was concerned, because in September 1965 the minions of 'the good Doctor' terminated the passenger service on the Lakeside branch. Of course it was losing money. It could not fail to do so thanks to the fat-headed, unimaginative way in which the service was organized. A shuttle service to and from Ulverston may have been all very well when the railway was the only way the great majority of travellers could get to Lakeside and the delightful steam yachts. But what about that eastern curve at Plumpton Junction? Think on it!

Eighteen months after the withdrawal of the passenger service the line was closed altogether, but immediately a private company, Lakeside Railway Estates, was formed to purchase the entire branch, up to and including the junction with the Furness main line at Plumpton. However,

the highway interests, which were engaged on some admittedly overdue development of the A590 through the Leven gorge, got in first. Had the railway remained south of Haverthwaite, something like a quarter of a million pounds would have been necessary to finance the improvements. And so the preservation scheme was watered down to no more than the three and a half miles of line between Haverthwaite and Lakeside, with the prospect of all rail connections with the rest of the national network being severed. Most of the locomotives and rolling stock wanted for the preserved line had been accumulated at Carnforth, on the site of the now-dismantled Furness Railway engine sheds, and when British Railways announced that they had let the contract for lifting the track between Haverthwaite and the Plumpton Junctions it became a matter of some urgency to move the stock while there were still rails on which it could run. While it is perhaps something of an exaggeration to suggest that 'cloak and dagger' methods had to be applied, two remarkable special trains slipped into Haverthwaite on 14 October 1970, the like of which had never been seen before.

The two major 'captures' from Carnforth were the ex-L M S 2-6-4 tanks 2073 and 2085, one of them oddly enough painted Caledonian blue. It has always been a source of surprise to me that these engines, and others of their kind, should be credited to C. E. Fairburn. It was rather like referring to the Furness 4-6-4 tanks as Rutherford's. It is true that Fairburn, a very eminent *electrical* engineer, was Chief Mechanical and Electrical Engineer of the L M S at the time some modifications were made to the standard 2-6-4 tank to increase its route availability; but the design remained 99.95 per cent Stanier, with the responsibility for the detailed alterations due to Ivatt, who was then Principal Assistant for Locomotives. However, all honour to the Lakeside and Haverthwaite Railway for having rescued these two fine engines from the scrap yard, and overnight the hitherto forlorn station yard at Haverthwaite became chock-a-block with locomotives and coaching stock. The two 2-6-4 tanks were reinforced by various little industrial engines, and in November 1970 the main line units were reinforced by a 'Black Five' 4-6-0, No. 44806, imported from Acrington.

Removal of the southern part of the original branch was completed in May 1971, but deliveries of further locomotives and rolling stock continued by road. When I had the pleasure of visiting the line again, at Easter 1980, the 'Black Five' had gone, but there were no fewer than fourteen locomotives, eleven of which were 'industrials'. It goes almost without saying that an immense amount of red tape had to be endured before authority was finally received to re-open the railway to passenger traffic, and it was not until May 1973 that the official ceremony took place, at Lakeside Station. There the occasion was graced by the presence of my great friend and co-author, the late and much lamented Bishop Eric Treacy. It was a happy thought to have the ceremony at Lakeside, rather than at Haverthwaite, for Lakeside retains the atmosphere of the original line to a marked degree, and the happy collaboration with 'Sealink', which now operates the Windermere Lake steamers, was manifest. The railway facilities in the station are somewhat reduced, but the lakeside pavilion still remains intact. The attractions it offers in the way of refreshments are now satisfying enough, though not quite so 'Edwardian' as when I first knew them.

In the Furness Railway time-table of 1906 to which I have already referred there is a whole-page advertisement for the pavilion, with a large photograph and the steam yacht *Tern* alongside. The advertisement stated that 'the Windermere Steam Yacht String Band will play on the Lakeside Pavilion daily during the Summer Months for Luncheon and for Afternoon Tea'. It was from this same photograph that A. Heaton Cooper worked up one of his delightful paintings, adding some swans on the lake and a larger and more animated crowd on the quayside than was apparent in the original photograph. The firm of Raphael Tuck & Son Ltd reproduced it as one of the coloured picture postcards one could buy for a

penny at stations on the Furness line. Apart from the refreshment pavilion the original signal box is still intact, together with at least one surviving example of a Furness Railway signal post.

The railway had no fewer than five locomotives in steam on the opening day: both the 2-6-4 tanks, which worked in double harness, the 'Black Five' 4-6-0 and two little 'saddle tanks'. One can understand the delight and pleasure of all those who had toiled for more than three years to bring the restoration of the line about; and even before the public service was fully inaugurated there came a very welcome boost, when the film company EMI hired the line for the day, and engine No. 2073 and a four coach train ran up and down while shots were made for the film of the children's book *Swallows and Amazons*. The line was honoured by the presence in the cast of no less distinguished an actress than Virginia McKenna. It was good to have such publicity at the very start of public operation. Since then the railway has carried increasing traffic, though it must be admitted that something of the old-time flavour of the li e has been lost. It is of course quite impossible to disregard the financial aspects of working, and that applies to the cost of locomotive fuel and maintenance and track repairs, as much as to the more obvious tasks of selling tickets to passengers.

The big 2-6-4 tanks, handsome and capable as they are, are not ideal units for a short shuttle service, and could quite easily involve an inordinate amount of coal simply to keep the firebars on their relatively large grates covered. Many years ago, when steam was in full possession of the East Coast main line, I remember getting involved with certain members of the locomotive running department over the relative coal consumption of the Gresley and Peppercorn 'Pacifics' on similar duties. One superintendent remarked to me that the latter were ideal if you had to take 600 tons on a dirty night; but he went on to emphasize that the day of 600-ton express trains, so common during the war, was fast receding, and with the big 50 sq. ft grates on the Peppercorns, fired thinly

Ex-L M S 2-6-4T No. 2085 in Caledonian colours with
C R coat of arms, at Haverthwaite, September 1972
Derek Cross

with hard coal, you very often had to fire just to keep the bars covered. In similar conditions with a Gresley you needed 25 per cent less coal! So it could easily be at Lakeside in comparing a 2-6-4 tank, with its 26.7 sq. ft of grate area, with a Hunslet 'Austerity' 0-6-0 saddle tank having a grate of only 16.8 sq. ft — and both engines have almost exactly the same nominal tractive effort.

As I've noted earlier, the Hunslets, of which there are two at Haverthwaite, may not be the

prettiest of engines, but as workhorses they are outstanding in their simplicity, strength and reliability. Of course the use of a modern general utility machine on a railway with such picturesque historical associations as the Lakeside line of the Furness Railway is the very negation of the idea that I expressed in the conclusion of *Branch Lines*, referred to in the Preface of the present book. Nevertheless, the short length and beautiful scenery of the Lakeside line tempts me to a few speculations as to how its unrivalled situation in one of the greatest tourist areas of the British Isles could be turned to exceptional historic as well as purely steam-nostalgic value. It was the sight of the yard at Haverthwaite, crowded with so many idle industrial locomotives, not to mention the two 2-6-4 tanks, that set me thinking on lines that will probably be regarded as pure heresy by those responsible when they first read this.

In these days, when so much of the original atmosphere of the lineside still remains, especially in the terminus at Lakeside, would it not be possible to have a full Furness Railway replica branch train? At the present time when working replicas of the *Rocket* and of *Sanspareil* have been constructed, and news has come from South Wales that a replica of the Pen-y-darren locomotive of 1904 is in hand, could not disposal of some of the unused locomotive power at Haverthwaite provide something towards the cost of building a replica Furness 2-4-2 tank for the Lakeside line? By all means retain the Hunslet 0-6-0 saddle tanks as the 'bread and butter' earning workhorses, but have a new little 2-4-2 to haul period trains, possibly at supplementary fares.

The idea of creating a genuine period atmosphere on a preserved railway is not new. It has been done in New Zealand and in the USA, and the size and situation of the Lakeside line seems to offer an exceptional opportunity in England.

The Hunslet 'Austerity' 0-6-0T *Cumbria* leaving Haverthwaite for Windermere (Lakeside), July 1978
David Eatwell

Another shot of the Hunslet 0-6-0T *Cumbria*, in March 1978, en route for Windermere (Lakeside)   *David Eatwell*

14

CARNFORTH STEAMTOWN

At the beginning of the 1920s Carnforth was a very busy railway centre. Except on the three daily through carriage services between Euston and the Furness line it seemed that everybody going to or from anywhere else had to change there. And except to a dedicated, single-minded railway enthusiast it was one of the dreariest, most unsalubrious spots one could imagine, The platform accommodation can be readily imagined from the situation today, except that an additional platform face has been added for down trains passing to the Furness and Midland lines, while those that once served the West Coast main line have had the facings removed and access to trains blocked off by fencing. In any case no West Coast main line trains now stop. One has to make connection with them at Lancaster.

'Change at Carnforth!' What memories those three words have for me: changes in so many senses. At that time all three companies working into the station had their own engine sheds. The Furness depot, quite a big affair with accommodation for about forty locomotives, was just abreast of the station, where the workshops of Steamtown now stand; but one could not see much of what was going on because of the wall that supported the roof covering in the sharply curved platform used by all Furness trains, and the running line alongside. The Furness Railway then had about 130 locomotives, and the great majority were concentrated at three sheds — Whitehaven (Corkickle), Barrow and Carnforth. The North Western sheds were a little to the south, alongside the main line. They were then almost entirely concerned with freight. The day had yet to come when they had the crack 'Ulster Express' working between Morecambe and Crewe.

When I first knew the place the Carnforth ironworks were still in operation. Its plant and soaring chimney were located in the space between the North Western main line and the encircling curve of the Midland line, from its short bay platform — in the form of 'a logarithmic spiral', as E. L. Ahrons once described it — to where it headed north-east over the bridge across the L N W R line. The Midland engine sheds were just beyond the bridge. They were concerned with relatively minor jobs, such as providing the shuttle service to Wennington by which some Midland trains connected with the Morecambe-West Riding semi-fasts. The line to Wennington was a joint concern of the Furness and Midland, and while the latter company provided locomotives and rolling stock, the stations were all built and equipped in the Furness style.

In the run down before the final abolition of steam trains on British Railways, Carnforth was one of the last outposts. The separate sheds were

Courses Provisional... available

	Subject		
1	English		
	Communication Studies		
	Mathematics		
2	Secretarial Studies		
	Food and Nutrition		
	Technical Craft/Wood		
3	French		
	Chemistry		
	Biology		
	Technical Drawing		
	Technical Craft/Metal		
	Food and Nutrition		
	Art		
4	Physics		
	Biology		
	German		
	Music		
	History		
	Modern Studies		
	Secretarial Studies		
	Social Studies		
5	Chemistry		
	Physics		
	Latin		
	Art		
	Geography		
	Accounting		
	Clerical & Office Skills		
	Metal Work		
	Woodwork *		
	Fabrics & Fashion *		
	Spanish *		

Tick... lank box.

Tick one blank box.

Tick one blank box.

In the following column students must take 5 units from those chosen above then chosen. Guidance is compulsory, and if H.English and/or H Maths is chosen above then they/it must be taken here.

	units available	units chosen
Guidance	1	1
P.E.	1 or 2	1
Art Appr.	1	1
Music Appr.	1	1
P.E.	1	1
Arithmetic 'O'	1	1
English 'O'	1	1
English 'H'	1	1
Mathematics 'H'	1	1
Community Service	2	
Computer Studies	1 or 2	1
Private Study	1	2
TOTAL		5

Mark number of units chosen opposi... subject.

They must total 5.

dispensed with in the big reorganization of the L M S motive power department in the mid-1930s when Carnforth became the parent shed for five sub-sheds, namely Barrow, Lakeside, Coniston, Oxenholme and Tebay. Then Carnforth put a new shed on the site of the former Furness depot. In the days when steam was banned entirely on British Railways several engines were collected at Carnforth with the idea of forming a north-western railways museum, to include certain celebrated Continental types. There was always the hope that the steam ban might eventually be lifted, and full advantage was taken of the repair facilities included in the 'new' L M S shed to make some of the 'orphans of the storm' serviceable to the extent of being able to steam up and down the yard. With the lifting of the ban and the selection of some routes through Carnforth as eligible for steam operation, what had begun as a museum became a steam motive power depot of some magnitude.

At roughly the same time the establishment of the National Railway Museum at York provided a collateral source of vintage motive power. The move to York was much criticized at the time, on account of its distance from the metropolis, but quite apart from the move having brought much additional excursion traffic to British Railways, the siting of the new museum with rail connection to the main line meant again that engines that were serviceable could be brought out and used for steam special trains. A happy spirit of collaboration developed, as it did with the smaller Steam Centres further south. Carnforth in particular became a strategic Steam Centre of the first importance. It was in direct line of communication with all the northern routes authorized for steam train operation, and with its large yard area its attractions could be extended to local activities as well as to provision of power for main line steam specials.

In a book of this kind one does not need to go into strict chronological sequence or precise dating, but I suppose that more than any other factor that brought Carnforth into the premium position it now holds was the rescue of the *Flying Scotsman* from its precarious impounding in California, after the financial disaster of its American tour. For with the *Flying Scotsman* came George Hinchcliffe, bringing with him valuable experience in maintaining and running steam locomotives in out-of-the-way conditions. I often recall the days long before he became involved with *Flying Scotsman*, when as a village schoolmaster in Lincolnshire he made some of my 'O' gauge model locomotives — how proud I am to have them today — but it was his work as Engineer and General Manager at Carnforth that transformed a venturesome and courageous enterprise into a solid, efficient, utterly reliable depot on which British Railways have been able to base their latest enterprises in running steam specials.

There is so much friendly interchange of motive power with the National Railway Museum at York that the uninitiated might wonder who owned which! One of my own earliest contacts with the modern Carnforth was at the time of the centenary celebrations of the Settle and Carlisle Railway in 1976. At that time the ban on steam had not been removed from the latter line, but the organizers had prepared a brave show with a steam-hauled special from Carnforth to Hellifield which would be taken to Carlisle by diesel. From Carnforth the special was to be hauled by two engines particularly associated with the Carlisle road in the past, the Midland Compound No. 1000 which, as M R No. 2631, went new to the line in 1902, and a 'Black Five', another old habitué of the road. Intending to make a gala weekend of it, my wife and I drove up from Bath on the Friday, but on arrival at Giggleswick we were horrified to learn that *both* Midland engines had failed. The sprightly little L N W R 2-4-0 *Hardwicke* was at Carnforth in spanking condition, but much more was needed for that heavy special, and we learned that arrangements were in hand to get *Flying Scotsman* across from York. So things eventuated; but as more than one enthusiast remarked how ironical it was that for so special a Midland occasion assistance had to be obtained from North Western and Great Northern engines!

The *Flying Scotsman* hauling the memorial train 'The Lord Bishop' on 30 September 1978 to Appleby for the service in honour of Bishop Eric Treacy who died there in May 1978. The author was a passenger in this train, here seen climbing the last mile to Aisgill summit

David Eatwell

The greatest triumph for Carnforth came in 1978. Hitherto the increasing number of steam-hauled specials had been privately chartered, organized and financed by one or another of the many enthusiast societies, but in 1978, thanks to the enterprise of the Passenger Marketing Manager of the London Midland Region, the very splendid 'Cumbrian Coast Express' was put on, not by one of the enthusiast societies but by British Railways themselves. British Railways had to hire the power to do the job from one or another of the private owners, but that they did so in cordiality and confidence was enough to show the status that George Hinchcliffe and his men at Carnforth, and their equally splendid counterparts at the National Railway Museum at York, had attained in the eyes of the management of British Railways.

It may seem that I am getting somewhat off the beam in writing of steam specials on the main lines of British Railways, even though the trains are hauled by privately owned steam locomotives. But is it not the dénouement, the goal to which so many of us have been looking and hoping: the resurrection, even if not more than a small part, of an era which few except the oldest amongst us can remember? Who can recall the days when *all* steam locomotives were clean? Between the two world wars most of the locomotives working crack expresses were reasonably clean, but as the drive to secure increased utilization developed, particularly on the L N E R the external appearance of many of the 'Pacifics' deteriorated into a sorry state. They may have been sound enough in wind and limb, but to outward appearances they were filthy. It was ironic that when the war came and train services were reduced at first, time was found to clean some of them up. But in later years, with

A delightful distant shot of *Hardwicke* crossing the Kent Viaduct at Arnside (Furness line) with a return excursion from Grange-over-Sands to Carnforth, in May 1976. Spectators line the shore to see the veteran pass   *David Eatwell* few exceptions, it became rare to see engines that were not grubby, to say the least of it.

However, it would now be unthinkable for any of the Steam Centres to put a locomotive on show that was not in immaculate condition. To me, who began train spotting more than seventy years ago, the continued interest is phenomenal. In the first year that the Cumbrian Coast Express ran I was favoured with a footplate pass. It was near the end of the season when interest might have worn off a little. It wasn't a particularly fine or sunny day, yet I am hardly exaggerating when I suggest that at least *one thousand* photographs of the train were taken on the trip from Carnforth to Sellafield and back!

The British Railways excursions in the North Country involve some locomotive assignments for the privately owned units that would have been considered unusual, if not exactly unsuitable, in the normal days of pre-diesel operation. The Furness line was never one over which really heavy passenger trains were run. Probably the heaviest was the incredibly beautiful 'white train' built by the L N W R for Edward VII, and decreed by him to have saloon interiors like a yacht. It was this train that brought George V and Queen Mary to see the wartime activities of the Furness district in 1917, and it was hauled by two of the Pettigrew 6 ft 4-4-0 engines of the '130' class. But even that heavy train was not to be compared with a 500-ton corridor excursion, booked non-stop from Carnforth to Ravenglass. Those excursions were booked to take the Barrow avoiding line which, in the up direction at any rate, is one of the most awkward pieces of railway to be found on any main line. The Furness main line originally had nothing to do with Barrow itself. It took a fairly straight course southward from Kirkby-in-Furness to Piel Pier, avoiding the hilly country of the Barrow isthmus by slipping through the oddly named 'Vale

Lord Nelson on the northbound Cumbrian Coast Express approaching Seascale, August 1980

John Titlow

152

Leander on tour: the southbound Cumbrian Coast Express, skirting Morecambe Bay between Grange-over-Sands and the Kent Viaduct, May 1979

John Titlow

of Deadly Nightshade' by Furness Abbey. When a branch to Dalton was added it was done by a very sharply curved and steeply graded single line.

It was this that eventually became part of the Barrow avoiding line, obviating the need to take heavy through mineral trains from the north through the crowded purlieus of Barrow itself. But such trains usually stopped at Park South to take rear end banking assistance round the curve of the avoiding line and up the subsequent heavy pull to Lindal Moor. The gradient is 1 in 100 throughout from Park South. Imagine a lengthy corridor express train of 450 or 500 tons negotiating this same stretch unassisted! The spectacle and the footplate experience will always remain vividly in my mind. The scene lies only a few miles from where my family home was for many years, and as I recall boyhood memories of those red Furness 0-6-0s pounding up round the curve with heavy loads of iron ore, I could not have then imagined that one day I would ride round that same curve on no lesser engine than the 'A4' Pacific *Sir Nigel Gresley*. What sights that curve can now present to the beholder, as the immaculately turned out, privately owned locomotives take their turns in working the British Railways specials: *Flying Scotsman*, *Lord Nelson* and one of the toughest of all 4-6-0s, *Leander*.

It is of particular pleasure to me that *Lord Nelson* has joined the engines regularly working from Carnforth, because I have an early morning memory of it that does not fade with the years. I had an engine pass to ride one of the famous Cunard Ocean Liner specials from Southampton. The liner *Queen Elizabeth* had brought so many passengers that there had to be three trains for Waterloo. *Lord Nelson* had the first of these, and I remember that as we backed down from Canute Road level crossing we came right beneath the bow of the great liner. It was an eerie feeling because by

---

A Southern visitor to Cumbria: the celebrated 4-6-0 No. 850 *Lord Nelson* crossing the Eskmeals Viaduct, south of Ravenglass, August 1980   *John Titlow*

Leander on the Settle and Carlisle line with the Cumbrian Mountain Express crossing Dent Head Viaduct. The smoke-filled north portal of Blea Moor tunnel can be seen just above the last coach of the train, April 1980

John Titlow

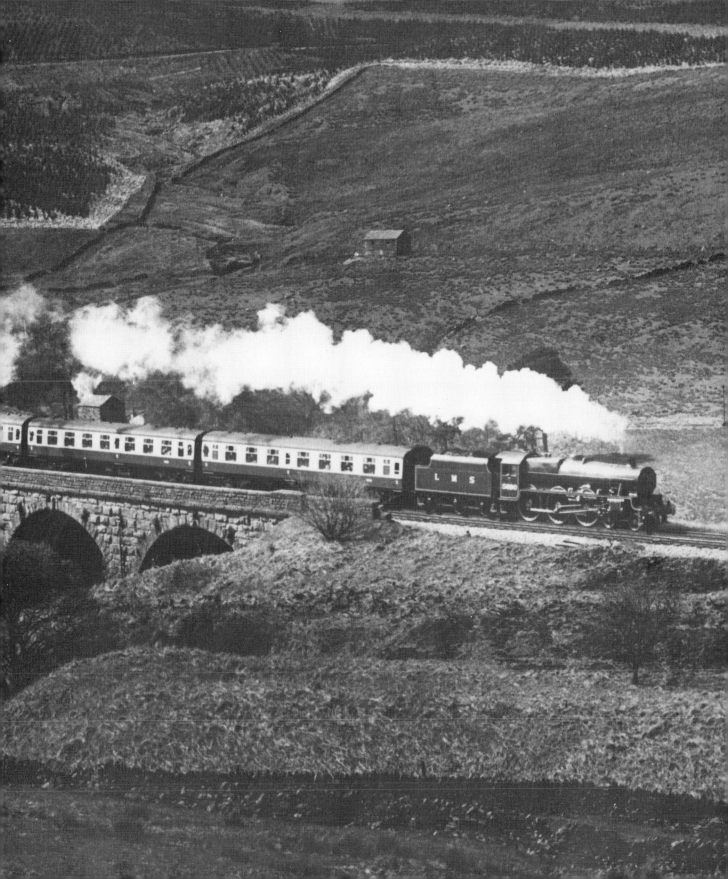

comparison our big locomotive seemed a mere toy. I wonder if Maunsell and his men ever looked forward to a day when their *chef d'oeuvre* would come pounding up the 1 in 100 gradients through the Dalton and Lindal tunnels with trains as heavy or even heavier than the boat trains for which it was designed, and over the grave where that Furness 0-6-0 No. 115 of immortal memory lies entombed. Incidentally, what a chance for an archaeological dig!

But — 'tell it not in Gath' — it seems from all accounts that it is *Leander* that has been stealing the show lately among the Carnforth stalwarts. I am not altogether surprised, because in my own experience on the footplate I don't think I have ever come across a 4-6-0 that for sheer 'guts' could surpass a Stanier Jubilee in fighting a mountain gradient. The original 'Scots' could be pretty good, but I am never likely to forget a wartime occasion when *Victoria* was put on in substitution for a 'Rebuilt Scot' on the up day express from St Enoch to London. Externally she was indescribably filthy, but my God what an engine! I only wish I had a tape recorder with me to register the noise as the Leeds driver flogged her from Kilmarnock up to the Mossgiel tunnel, or from Carlisle on the great banks of the Settle and Carlisle line. I have recorded in *Main Lines across the Border* how consistently she steamed against such vigorous treatment.

And mention of the Settle and Carlisle brings me to the latest enterprise of the London Midland Region using privately owned steam locomotives — the grandly imaginative 'Cumbrian Mountain Express'. I think that all of us who had any hand in the centenary celebrations of the Settle and Carlisle line had pangs of disappointment that the rules then in operation could not be bent, ever so slightly, so as to allow steam locomotives to approach, if not actually to enter, the Citadel station at Carlisle; but B R has made ample amends since, with the round trips of the Cumbrian Mountain Express. Some years ago when I was travelling in Canada I was enthralled by the 'Winter Wonderland' excursion trips run by

the Algoma Central Railway to view, in the grip of mid-winter, some of the most spectacular canyon scenery, when lakes were completely frozen over and raging waterfalls frozen solid. I was reminded of this one day when I was a passenger on the Cumbrian Mountain Express. From Preston we were going north direct, over Shap, and oddly enough the weather conditions were the reverse to what one usually expects in these wild mountain regions. For it was the Lancashire plain and the West Coast route that were deep in drifting snow, not that it made any difference to the progress of our electrically hauled train. But when we got north of Shap the weather cleared, and our return ride, with glorious sunshine lighting the snow-covered lands of the Settle and Carlisle line, was the sheerest delight.

Ever since the grouping of the railways in 1923 the Settle and Carlisle has been a testing route *par excellence* for different locomotive types. But in those early days which began right back in the late autumn of 1923, so little was known about these tests, even in railway circles, that to my knowledge not a single photograph was taken; and the spectacle of Midland, London and North Western, and Caledonian locomotives blasting their way up to Aisgill, with what would have been considered as gross overloads by current Midland standards, must have been enthralling. The time of day was no excuse on the up journey for the tests were made on the 12.10 p.m. up from Carlisle. In mid-winter, however, the return runs were made after dark. It was much the same with the B R tests made after nationalization: a few snapshots by individual members of the dynamometer crews and that was all.

Today the running of the privately owned locomotives on the Cumbrian Mountain Express is being magnificently documented, not only on the

At Carnforth: the French ex-P L M Pacific No. 231-K-22 during a Saturday afternoon 'steam-up' in March 1976, in which a German 'Pacific' also took part
David Eatwell

Settle and Carlisle line itself, in all its scenic grandeur, but in the connecting runs across to Carnforth from Skipton. This has been a particular pleasure to me, because it was a line I knew especially well as a boy in my end of term journeys between Barrow and Giggleswick. Between Settle Junction and Wennington there is some splendid scenery including perhaps the finest of all views of Ingleborough. So, in all its increasing activities one can shout 'Floreat Carnforth'!

The one very slight regret is that they cannot use, beyond yard limits, those two tremendous Continental 'Pacifics', the French 231K and the German '01'. After the immortal Chapelons, the ex-P L M 231K was perhaps the most famous and successful of all French 'Pacific' locomotives. The 'K' was a very successful modernization of the 'C' class four-cylinder compound of 1912, with high degree superheat, twin orifice blastpipe and greatly improved and internally streamlined steam passages. The 'K' class 4-6-2s put up some magnificent performances in the later steam days on the French railways, and I witnessed a number of them personally. The preserved engine at Carnforth makes a breathtaking sight and an interesting contrast to the other giant museum piece, the German '01' Pacific.

And so, at Carnforth, I conclude the story. There are many other private railways in operation, or in contemplation in this country, but I have written only of the standard gauge lines.

However, I cannot end without paying a resounding tribute to the enterprise and dedication of the men who have made all this possible. It is one thing to be a railway enthusiast, to photograph trains at the lineside, to browse over railway books, to join in tours and winter meetings; but it is quite another to spend a great deal of one's spare time doing strictly disciplined 'hard labour' jobs out on the line, in workshops, or even in the relatively unglamorous operational duties. The private railways of Great Britain, and those who work on them with such dedication, have carved a niche for themselves in the Hall of Fame that one imagines exists in the mind of all who have railways at heart.

I know there are some who would deride the whole activity as that of a crowd of overgrown schoolchildren 'playing trains'; but the volunteers are keeping alive the memory of a great epoch. The invention, development, and prowess of the steam locomotives were the consummation of the Industrial Revolution in Britain — the invention that matched the evolution of machinery of all kinds with rapid, reliable, and relatively cheap transport for everyone. The steps that have now been taken to preserve working examples of this great epoch represent a vital contribution to national history.

Index

A heavy 'Santa Special' moving away from Haworth
on the last stage of the climb to Oxenhope, hauled by
two American-type locomotives: 2-8-0 No. 5828
leading and 0-6-0T next to the train, December 1978

David Eatwell